Sampling the Book

Sampling the Book

Renaissance Prologues and the French *Conteurs*

Deborah N. Losse

Lewisburg
Bucknell University Press
London and Toronto: Associated University Presses

© 1994 by Associated University Presses, Inc.

All rights reserved. Authorization to photocopy items for internal or personal use, or the internal or personal use of specific clients, is granted by the copyright owner, provided that a base fee of $10.00, plus eight cents per page, per copy is paid directly to the Copyright Clearance Center, 27 Congress Street, Salem, Massachusetts 01970. [0-8387-5244-6/94 $10.00+8¢ pp, pc.]

Associated University Presses
440 Forsgate Drive
Cranbury, NJ 08512

Associated University Presses
25 Sicilian Avenue
London WC1A 2QH, England

Associated University Presses
P.O. Box 338, Port Credit
Mississauga, Ontario
Canada L5G 4L8

The paper used in this publication meets the requirements of the American National Standard for Permanence of Paper for Printed Library Materials Z39.48-1984.

Library of Congress Cataloging-in-Publication Data

Losse, Deborah N., 1944–
    Sampling the book : Renaissance prologues and the French conteurs / Deborah N. Losse.
      p.   cm.
    Includes bibliographical references and index.
    ISBN 0-8387-5244-6
    1. French fiction—16th century—History and criticism—Theory, etc. 2. Authors and readers—France—History—16th century. 3. French fiction—16th century—Criticism, Textual. 4. Prologues and epilogues—History and criticism. 5. Short stories, French— Criticism, Textual. 6. Authority in literature. 7. Transmission of texts. 8. Books—France—Format. 9. Renaissance—France. 10. Literary form. I. Title.
PQ643.L67   1994
843'.309—dc20   92-55052
                                                                                  CIP

PRINTED IN THE UNITED STATES OF AMERICA

Contents

Acknowledgments	7
Introduction	11
1. From *Auctor* to *Auteur:* Authorization and Appropriation in the Renaissance	19
2. *Nue vérité ou invention poétique?* History and Fiction in the Prologue of the Renaissance *Nouvelle*	33
3. Sampling the Book: Beginning Metaphors and Their Poetic Function	46
4. The Functions of the Prologue: A Renaissance View	57
5. Bridging the Gap: The Transition to the Main Text	79
6. Women Addressing Women—The Differentiated Text	90
Afterword	101
Notes	104
Select Bibliography	122
Index	129

Acknowledgments

Many people have given me help and support in the long process of writing this book. I wish to acknowledge their advice and encouragement but take responsibility for any shortcomings in the study that follows. The idea for the project grew out of a seminar devoted to satire in the works of Rabelais and Cervantes which I taught with Edward H. Friedman, now Professor of Spanish at Indiana University. A summer seminar, sponsored by the National Endowment for the Humanities and under the direction of François Rigolot, gave me a significant start in beginning to conceptualize the form and content of the project. I would like to express my thanks to Professor Rigolot for his guidance in the early stages of the study. My former colleague Theodore Cachey, now at the University of Notre Dame, helped me in tracing the origins of Italian liminary form.

In the latter stages of the project, Joan A. Buhlmann (University of Nebraska), Stephen G. Nichols (Johns Hopkins University), Diane S. Wood (Texas Tech University), Elizabeth Wright (San Francisco State University), Colette H. Winn (Washington University) have made invaluable suggestions for improvement in individual chapters. I was able to try out early versions of three chapters at the Annual Meeting of the Modern Language Association in New Orleans in a session directed by Edwin Duval, at an international conference "European Renaissance: National Traditions" held at the University of Glasgow, and at the annual conference of the Rocky Mountain MLA.

Arizona State University has been generous in its support of my research. An Arts/Sciences/Humanities Grant provided travel funds for research at the Bibliothèque Nationale in Paris, and a grant from Women's Studies and the College of Liberal Arts enabled me to complete the chapter devoted to the prologues of women authors. I would also like to thank my research assistant, Nadia Chihani, for her help in tracking down and photocopying hundreds of articles.

Before concluding, let me express my appreciation to the editors of

Medievalia at Humanistica, Symposium, and *Neophilologus* for granting permission to include portions of articles published in their journals. The editors at Bucknell University Press and at Associated University Presses have been extremely helpful and considerate. Finally, I thank my colleagues in French and in other languages at Arizona State University and the past and present Chairs of the Department of Foreign Languages, Peter Horwath and Pier R. Baldini. But I could not have seen the project to completion without the support and affection of my family. It is to John, Kate, and Owen that I dedicate this book.

* * *

I have obtained permission to use portions of the following articles:

"From Auctor to Auteur: Authorization and Appropriation in the Renaissance." *Medievalia et Humanistica* New Series 16 (1988): 153–63.

"Sampling the Book. Beginning Metaphors and their Poetic Function." *Neophilologus* 73 (1990): 192–201.

"Nue vérité ou invention poétique? History and Fiction in the Prologues of the Renaissance Conteurs." *Symposium* (1989): 107–17.

An earlier and different version of "Women Addressing Women" appears in a volume entitled *Renaissance Women Writers: French Texts: American Contexts*, edited by Anne R. Larsen and Colette H. Winn, to be published by Wayne State University Press.

Sampling the Book

Introduction

Approach

When literary historians look back on the year 1987, they may well view it as the year of the preface. The first months of the year saw the publication of Gérard Genette's *Seuils,* a lengthy study of various forms of paratexts (preface, afterword, epigraph) as well as the publication of a special issue of the French journal *Poétique* (no. 69), devoted to the paratext.[1] In the Autumn of the same year, the American journal *L'Esprit Créateur* brought out a special issue entitled *The Preface (Ouvertures, Prolégomènes, Préludes, Avis, Avant-propos).*[2] Two years later, the Swiss periodical *Versants* published an issue devoted to sixteenth century prologues.[3] How do we explain the sudden renewal in interest in a genre or sub-genre long considered by many writers to be a tiresome but necessary part of the book's formal appearance?

A conventional embellishment, necessary at least in the early years of printing to the physical appearance of the work, the preface to the narrative work is, nevertheless, that part of the book that even attentive readers are apt to skim over or skip completely in their haste to get to the "main" text. They may come back to the preface after reading the work, but the fact remains that in the past century or so, the preface is simply not viewed as an integral part of the text it escorts into the world.[4]

In the one area in which the prologue is perceived as an integral part of the narrative work—in part because in the *chanson de geste* and in the Medieval romance there is often no textual separation between liminary text and the main text—comprehensive studies on the prologue as genre have flourished. Medieval scholars such as Tony Hunt, A. J. Minnis, Michel Zink, Marie-Louise Ollier, Pierre-Yves Badel, and James Schultz among others, have sought to define major elements of the Medieval Prologue.[5]

In the Renaissance, the prologue and main text continue to be interdependent parts of the same narrative enterprise. Rabelais's prologues provide an initiation for the reader into the fictional world of the author. In his *Nouvelles Récréations et Joyeux Devis*, Bonaventure Des Périers discourages his reader from skipping over the *préambule* by making it a part of his first tale. Only towards the end of the sixteenth century do authors begin to express cynicism about the efficacy of prefatory discourse—a cynicism that becomes commonplace in later centuries in the works of such authors as Flaubert, Gautier, and Mallarmé. Tabourot, writing in 1583, reproaches prefatory practices such as flattering a wealthy patron, threatening would-be critics, citing learned authorities to cover up individual shortcomings: "Je n'ay voulu toutesfois estre imitateur de telles façons de faire, que j'ay de tout temps estimé vaines et ridicules" [I sought not to imitate, however, those ways of doing things, which I have always thought to be fruitless and silly].[6] Tabourot's contemporary, Montaigne, condemns the emphasis on frivolous, non-substantive liminary devices: "Les lettres de ce temps sont plus en bordures et prefaces, qu'en matiere" [The letters of this age consist more in embroideries and preambles than in substance] (*Essais* I, 40, 247; 186–87).[7] The immediate context of his remark concerns epistolary form, although a subsequent comment at the end of the paragraph and character confirms its application to humane letters, "Je trouve pareillement de mauvaise grâce d'en charger le front et inscription des livres que nous faisons imprimer" [I also consider it in bad taste to load with these the frontispiece and title page of the books we print] (*Essais* I, 40, 248; 187).

Renaissance printing practices greatly altered the appearance of the book's front matter. In *L'Apparition du livre*, Lucien Febvre and Henri-Jean Martin confirm Montaigne's observation on the crowding of the liminary pages of the book. They speak of the gradual elongation of the title in the first half of the sixteenth century and of the care to fill the entire title page with a greatly expanded book title with even a short inventory of the book's contents.[8] Contemporary interest in Renaissance printing practices explains in part the current renewal of interest in the preface and in other aspects of the paratext.

To find a second explanation, one might point to the application of speech act theory to textual analysis. With its ties to the circumstances of enunciation in both classical oratory (the exordium) and in the Greek and Latin theater (*parodos* or *parodus*), the preface must be viewed in its performative light.[9] Reworking the *Rhetorica ad Heren-*

nium and Cicero's *De inventione*, Brunetto Latini tells us in the thirteenth century *Livres dou Trésor*, that the prologue strives to secure the goodwill [*bienvaillance*], the attention [*volonté d'oïr*], and the curiosity or interest [*volonté de savoir*] of the public.[10] Viewing the preface as a dynamic interaction between interlocutors—one which can not be understood independently of the speech act itself—modern theoreticians have restored life to these documents once considered a kind of inert form located at the start of the work.

Written as they were in the century or so following the invention of printing, Renaissance prologues give us one of the few opportunities to observe how men and women writers of the period adapted to the changes and innovations in the circulation of the book.[11] New modes of circulation brought about changes in liminary conventions; the prologue became a locus of mediation between an artist, anxious about the rapidly expanding public, and an audience, whose tastes were evolving and diversifying.[12]

The tradition of short narrative form—the *conte* or *nouvelle*—flourished throughout the French Renaissance. The word *conte*, as used by Renaissance storytellers, refers more appropriately to the *nouvelle*, the account of an event tied to the daily events of a social group in a specific time and place. The *nouvelle*, is associated with a recent, newsworthy occurrence, although it may be in fact have its origins in older sources.[13] The expectations of the sixteenth century readers set limits on the author's creative inclination—namely that the material appear to be recent and anchored in everyday life, and secondly, that the artist give a new look to the source material [*matière*], received from a reliable source or eye witness. To this end, the prologuist of the *Cent Nouvelles Nouvelles*, a work which so influenced the development of the *conte*, praises his work as being of quite recent date ["d'assez fresche memoire"] and having a very new look ["de myne beaucoup nouvelle"].[14]

The prologues of individual *conteurs* have long attracted critical interest, and yet a full-length comprehensive study of the prologues of French storytellers has yet to be done.[15] The present study is comprehensive in that it selects a variety of prologues to both short and long narrative tales spanning the sixteenth century. Among the authors represented are Philippe de Vigneulles, Des Périers, Hélisenne de Crenne, Jeanne Flore, Marguerite de Navarre, Noël du Fail, Louise Labé, Jacques Yver, Philippe Le Picard writing under the name of Philippe d'Alcripe, Bénigne de Poissenot, Cholières,

Bouchet, Tabourot, and Béroalde de Verville. To embark on a study of the prefaces of the Renaissance without including Rabelais and Montaigne would be to overlook two of the major influences in the development of prefatory discourse. Their prologues have been studied in great depth elsewhere, and I shall draw salient points from these studies where appropriate. The aim of my study is to set their liminary discourse within the larger context of prefatory strategies used by the French *conteurs*. Like all satirical works, the Rabelaisian chronicles are a hybrid form of which the narrative tale is but one element. The generic classification of Montaigne's *Essais* proves an even greater challenge, but from the time he first published his works, the *conteurs* counted Montaigne as one of them.

Efforts to show how the *essai* evolved from the short narrative form have persisted since Vianey's article, "Montaigne conteur," in 1940 and even before.[16] It is without doubt Gabriel A. Pérouse, distinguished for his numerous studies on the evolution of a short narrative form, who makes the best case for Montaigne's inclusion as part practitioner and theorist of the *genre narratif bref*. Given the diverse tendencies of short narrative form, Pérouse explains that Montaigne has simply pushed the open form of the tale to its logical extension, and in so doing, creates the essay.[17] The elastic form of the *conte* allowed for such a natural evolution. Pérouse cites Montaigne's use of both extensive and succinct narrated illustrations of philosophical and ethical points along with his indifference as to whether the same illustrations are true or merely plausible as evidence of his affinity to the methods of the *conteurs*. The fact that he intermingles discursive segments with narrative segments—a common practice among the *conteurs* in the period around 1580—illustrates quite clearly Montaigne's status as a *conteur*. That Montaigne's imitators, such as François Le Poulchre de la Motte Messemé, perceived him as a *conteur* as much as a philosopher is evident in their borrowing elements from narrative segments of the *Essais*. For the storytellers who followed him, Montaigne's essays were in fact moralizing narratives—a variant or offshoot of the *conte*.[18] It is not suprising, then, that his notice "au lecteur" should influence the prefaces of his fellow *conteurs*, just as the prologues of his storytelling predecessors would influence his own liminary style.

The focus of the analysis is not so much the historic circumstances in which the prologues were written, but the emergence of specific liminary strategies. How do sixteenth century storytellers adapt or change the Medieval practice of authorization? What is the interrelationship between history and fiction in the Renaissance prologue? What types of metaphors appear or recur in the prologue, and what role do they play in setting up a "good reading" of the text that follows? Do the functions carried out in the prefatory space differ greatly from those used in the prefaces of later periods, as outlined in Genette's extensive list of prefatory functions? What techniques does the Renaissance storyteller use to ease the transition between his prefatory remarks and the opening of the "main" text? Finally, do women practicing the short narrative form use the same liminary strategies as their male counterparts or can we distinguish a marked woman's discourse [*discours de femme*] in their prologues? The present study explores these questions through the analysis of the prefatory remarks of selected storytellers of sixteenth century France.

Definitions of Prefatory Terms

Prefatory statements bear various labels in French: *proème* [proem], *préambule* [preamble], *prologue*, *prolégomènes* [proloegomena], *avant-propos* [foreword], *avis au lecteur* [notice to the reader], to name the most common. Genette classes all such terms under one global heading—*préface*.[19] Although the storytellers of the French Renaissance used prefatory labels somewhat interchangeably, it is clear that their Italian predecessors demanded more precision in the use of such terms. The *Dizionario etimologico della lingua italiana* offers some insights into the finer distinctions. Citing F. da Buti from around 1406, the *Dizionario etimologico* defines preamble [*preàmbolo*] as the introductory words of a discourse, treatise, or work.[20] In his letter to Cangrande della Scala, Dante underscores Aristotle's distinction between the *prooemium* [proem], reserved for oratory, and the prologue, used to introduce a poetic work.[21] He goes on to say that the prologuist speaks sometimes in the manner of the orator and sometimes in the manner of a poet. He offers the example of the prologue to the *Paradiso*, in which in the Ciceronian manner, he seeks first the goodwill, attention, and interest of the audience, and then invokes the aid of Apollo for inspiration (*Tutte le opere:* p. 347). But Dante does not always follow the Aristotelian distinction between the prologue and proem, for in his explanation of the second *canzone* of the *Convivio*, he refers to the opening of the verse *canzone* as a proem ("Trattato terzo," *Convivio, Tutte le opere:* p. 141). The etymological link between the preamble and *prooemium,* concerns movement: *preambulare,* to walk before; *pro,* in front of; *oimos,* road, way (*Dizionario etimologico,* 4: p. 967, p. 998). Prologue, on the other hand, is not associated with movement, but with speech: *pro,* before; *logos,* speech or discourse. Brunetto Latini connects the prologue to the introductory monologue of a theatrical work, a meaning that continued into the sixteenth century (*Dizionario etimologico,* 4: p. 987). Boccaccio, ever mindful of Dante, seems to respect the distinction made by his predecessor between the prologue (used in poetry) and the proem (used in prose) when he calls the preface to the *Decameron* a *proemio.* He follows to the letter the structure for prefatory discourse outlined by Dante in the letter to Cangrande della Scala. Boccaccio's *proemio* is a meeting of the thoughts of Cicero, as reflected in *De inventione,* and the reworking of Cicero by Dante. In describing his personal suffering, Boccaccio aims at earning the goodwill of his reader. To Dante's claim that good will can be acquired by promising material useful to the reader, Boccaccio promises to help those in need—the ladies who hide their love and remain cooped up in the small, confined space of their rooms ["nel piccolo circuito delle loro camere racchiuse dimorano"].[22] In response to Dante's statement that the promise of extraordinary events captures the reader's attention, Boccaccio outlines not only the depth of his own suffering in love, but promises tales and verses evoking the pleasurable and bitter aspects of love ["piacevoli e aspri casi d'amore"]. And finally, Boccaccio reworks Dante's notion of possibility [*possibilità*], in which the writer writes of things that may occur to the audience in the future in order to get them ready to hear the message (Dante, *Epistole, Tutte le opere:* p. 347). Boccaccio writes not for ordinary women, for whom spinning and sewing provide adequate entertainment, but for women who love, to whom his words may bring help and relief [in soccorso e rifugio di quelle che amano,] (*Decameron, Opere:* p. 8).

Ending with an invocation to Love, that Love may help him win the favor of the ladies to whom he is writing, Boccaccio again follows Dante's example (Dante, *Epistole, Tutte le opere:* p. 346). Dante makes a point that the invocation follows the *captatio benevolentiae* in the *Paradiso.* Boccaccio departs from the master in two respects in his *proemio* to the *Decameron.* Dante elaborates on the role of the humility motif in his *Convivio* (III, II), where he speaks of his unworthiness to treat his subject (*Tutte le opere:* p. 141). Although Boccaccio speaks of his lowly state [bassa condizione] in the *proemio*, he neglects mention of his inability to treat his subject. In another light, Boccaccio's *proemio* assumes the role of the *prologo* in the theater, "narrative monologue . . . designed to familiarize the audience with the myth that was the subject of the tragedy and with the circumstances of the action."[23] The author of the *Decameron* presents his characters, describes the pestilence which has given rise to the storytelling, and tells the audience what types of stories to expect. In short, his final paragraph eases the transition to the story of the plague besieging Florence and to the description of the virtuous circle of friends.

In this brief overview of labels assigned to prefatory remarks, we should note not only the importance of the Le Maçon translation of Boccaccio's *Decameron* in 1545 and its influence on Marguerite de Navarre and the other *conteurs*, but also the fact that Le Maçon translates the term *proemio* by *prologue*.[24] Among the *conteurs*, the term *proème* has little currency. Rabelais and Marguerite stick to the term *prologue*, but their contemporary, Bonaventure Des Périers uses *préambule* in his *Nouvelles Récréations et Joyeux Devis*. Estienne Tabourot entitles the first liminary remarks to the *Bigarrures du Seigneur des Accords* a *préface*, a term less current than the more popular *prologue* but at the end of his *préface*, in a conversational style of address to his reader, he reverts to the more familiar term, *prologue:* "Or il suffira pour ceste heure, car je voy bien que tu t'ennuyes d'un si long prologue" [Now that will suffice for the time being, for I see that you are bored by such a long prologue].[25] The preferred label among the *conteurs*, however, is a variation on the term *au lecteur* [to the reader]. Du Fail's *Propos rustiques* begins "Maistre Leon Ladulfi au lecteur." Hélisenne de Crenne speaks "aux lisantes" [to the lady readers], Cholières, "aux liseurs" [to the readers] and Bouchet "à Messieurs les Marchands de la ville de Poictiers" [To Messieurs the Merchants of the city of Poitiers]. Montaigne's decision to address his opening remarks "au lecteur" reflects a well-established French preference in prefatory labels. One might have expected Jacques Amyot to revive the more serious *proème* for the preface to his translation of Plutarch's *Vies des hommes illustres*.[26] Instead, he addresses "aux lecteurs" a highly instructional preface devoted to explaining the finer distinctions between *histoire* [history] and *vie* [life].

Conter—to tell tales—highlights the oral transmission of tales. And yet, within a century of the invention of the printing press, the *conteur* had given up a prefatory label which reaffirmed the connection between the tale and the spoken word (*pro* + *logos; prae* + *fari*—both *logos* and *fari* referring to speech) in favor of a label which reached only those who could read the printed word. In their prefatory titles *au lecteur, aux lecteurs, aux lisantes, aux liseurs,* the storytellers exclude the listener whose good will, attention, and right disposition their classical and medieval predecessors had sought to please. Only those initiated into the secrets of the printed text are invited to sample the liminary treasures of the majority of Renaissance tales. After Rabelais, Des Périers, and Marguerite de Navarre, the foreword [prologue], a circular form of discourse open to all, loses ground to the more exclusive channel of communication between author and reader.

1

From *Auctor* to *Auteur:* Authorization and Appropriation in the Renaissance

A source of controversy in contemporary scholarship on the Medieval prologue concerns the role played by classical rhetorical theory in its development. Tony Hunt documents instances in which the Arthurian prologue follows the structure of the exordium described in the *Rhetorica ad Herennium*, in Cicero's *De inventione*, and in Quintilian's *Institutio oratoria*. A. J. Minnis focuses on similarities between the academic prologues developed by Donatus, Remigius of Auxerre, Boethius, Saint Thomas Aquinas and the Medieval literary prologues of Jean de Meun, Chaucer, and Boccaccio. Minnis and Hunt stress the continuity between academic theory and literary practice.[1]

Other scholars, including Marie-Louise Ollier, Michel Zink, and James A. Schultz, are concerned with the development of the individual creative voice of the author in late twelfth and early thirteenth century romance, and fear that efforts to view the medieval prologues as applications of classical and medieval rhetorical theory fail to account for innovations resulting from experimentation with new and emerging literary genres. As perhaps the most outspoken critic of this practice, James A. Schultz comments: "To apply such doctrines to medieval prologues does not, from a purely logical standpoint, make any sense at all. In the second place, the precepts of the classical and medieval treatises are substantially at odds with the majority of actual vernacular prologues. The prologues violate classical rhetorical teaching as often as they follow it"[2] New genres, in this case romance and shorter narrative forms, demand and create new liminary structures in which the innovators question existing narrative practice and yet express concern about the future reception of their work.

My object in bringing up this controversy is not to add fuel to the fire, but to point out that two centuries later, we are faced with the same controversy. Narrative forms continue to develop, and the author is still faced with the choice between grounding his material solidly in past tradition and allowing the unique voice of the text to emerge. Through the *studia humanitatis*, classical rhetoric had gained an even greater stronghold on literary practice, both conscious and subconscious. Yet, we are again at a time of great literary innovation, and so, while we cannot ignore the influence of classical and Medieval liminary practices in the sixteenth century, the present study will explore changes in the ways in which Renaissance writers authorize their material and allow their own voice to emerge in the prologue. I recognize with Marie-Louise Ollier "the necessity of situating every text at the confluence of its own organization and of the tradition, or as a singular form in a literary space populated by other forms."[3] Such an approach neither ignores the literary or historical context in which the work was produced, nor betrays the internal structure and integrity of the work.

What is meant by authorization and appropriation? And more importantly, how were these terms understood in the later Middle Ages and in the early Renaissance? The authorization was very much connected with the notion of *auctor*—"an accolade bestowed on a popular writer by those late scholars and writers who used extracts from his works as sententious statements or *auctoritas*, gave lectures on his works in the form of commentaries, or employed them as literary models."[4] Only those authors said to have produced works of intrinsic worth were referred to as *auctores*. The authors of the *Roman de Thèbes*, the *Roman d'Alexandre*, and the *Roman de Troie* saw themselves more as translators who made the glories of antiquity accessible to those who did not read Latin. The term *roman* was first associated with the translation and adaptation of the Latin book into the vulgar tongue.[5] The authority comes not from the individual efforts of the translator or compiler, but from the intrinsic value of the source and the labors of those who have contributed to the *matière*. The faithful adapter gains credit through his respect for the source and the historical accuracy with which he writes. His reluctance to appropriate the narrative for himself, to make it a function of his own individual experience, increases his importance as the transmitter of the *estoire*, the source worthy of belief.[6]

Self-effacement in the job of faithfully transcribing source material does not prevent Benoît de Sainte-Maure from taking credit for what is his own contribution to the *Roman de Troie*. He is the first to tell the story of Troy in French, and he claims to shape, polish, and arrange the words much as a stone mason would prepare the stones of a building.[7]

With Chrétien de Troyes and his successors, authority begins to pass from the past and the source, to the present and the work in progress. In his preface to *Erec et Enide,* Chrétien points out the weakness of his source, a *conte d'aventure* without merit, and praises his own efforts to create a work which will last as long as Christianity.[8] The emphasis has shifted from the authority of past sources to the future reception of the text. With Chrétien, the prologue becomes a locus of self-advertisement, where the author/narrator affirms his authority to speak and makes a case for the present and future merit of what he has to say. We shall see that the play of tense, dominated by the narrative present but permitting glimpses into the past and future, is one of the principal qualities of the prologue emerging in the Renaissance.[9]

An element of play creeps into the strategy of authorization, as Jean de Meun, Chaucer, and Boccaccio stress their role as compiler— one who merely arranges the material and who has no responsibility for its content.[10] If Jean de Meun disclaims all responsibility for the antifeminist strain of his discourse, Chaucer apologizes for the rustic speech of his pilgrims, and Boccaccio blames the poor narrative techniques of his ladies. To alter the style would be to misrepresent the source material.

From authorizing the text through the use of predetermined sources and creditable *auctores,* the writer gradually begins to claim credit for his role in producing the source material. References to the *auctores* begin to appear along with the author's own name; the process of self-authorization begins as the author calls attention to individual efforts.[11]

Such prominent coupling of the authoritative source and the appropriating voice which characterizes the works bridging the late medieval period and the early Renaissance is evident in the *Cent Nouvelles Nouvelles* of Philippe de Vigneulles, composed in 1505. The prologue, whose first part is missing, evokes first the "vaillant auteur" [valiant author] who had collected the earlier and more famous *Cent Nouvelles Nouvelles,* and then the author of the new volume, "moy Philippe de Vigneulle, marchans de drap et simple d'entendement" [I, Philippe de Vigneulles, cloth merchant and man of simple understanding].[12] The authoritative text receives top billing, but then is abandoned in the process of explaining the generating circumstances of the present and more immediate volume of stories, gathered not in a Burgundian military barracks nor by gentlemen soldiers, but by Philippe himself in the "noble city of Metz." The connection, once made, gives way to disengagement and distancing as the author underscores his singular contribution to the genre—in Philippe's case, his status as able narrator ["bon facteur"] capable of turning everyday events into worthy material for a book "aussi bon que ceulx qui ont esté faict devant" [as good as those which were composed before] (*Cent Nouvelles Nouvelles:* p. 58).

What vestiges remain in the sixteenth century either as serious reminders of the Medieval practice of authorization, or as a parody of this practice? Weimann points out how "in places like Lyon, Strassburg, Frankfurt, London, and Madrid, wherever the connection with a growing market for the products of the printing press affected the property status of his discursive practice," the Renaissance author was faced with a broader repertoire of "ideological norms and literary choices" no longer bound to the expectations of a single social group or profession.[13] With this new flexibility, the authors sacrificed some of the security they had known when texts were addressed to a well-defined public with highly predictable literary tastes.

The flexible means of dealing with the issues of authorization and appropriation are immediately apparent in two prologues written within a few years of one another: the prologue to Rabelais's *Gargantua* (1534–35) and the first novella in the form of a preamble ["en forme de préambule"] introducing Des Periers's *Nouvelles Récréations et Joyeux Devis*, written before the author's death in 1544 and perhaps as early as 1538.[14] The famous *incipit* to the *Gargantua* prologue reveals Rabelais's affinity to the Medieval genres he is parodying:

> Beuveurs tres illustres, et vous, Verolez tres precieux,—car à vous, non à aultres, sont dediez mes escriptz,—Alcibiades, ou dialoge de Platon intitulé *Le Bancquet*, louant son precepteur Socrates, sans controverse prince des philosophes, entre aultres parolles le dict estre semblable es Silenes.[15]

> [Most noble boozers, and you my very esteemed and poxy friends—for to you and (not to others) are my writings dedicated—when Alcibiades, in the dialogue of Plato's entitled the Symposium, praises his master Socrates, beyond all doubt the prince of philosophers, he compares him, amongst other things, to a Silenus.]

In his typology of the common forms of *incipit* in the Medieval romances, Pierre-Yves Badel characterizes the second type by its call to attention and address to a chosen public.[16] Based on the Ciceronian notions of obtaining the condition of *benevolentia, docilitas,* and *attentio* in his audience, the narrator appeals to the learning and culture of the readers while flattering them. If the replacement of the more traditional *seigneurs* [lords] by *beuveurs* and *verolez* [boozers and poxy friends] calls attention to the playful rhetorical innovation of the narrator, his mention of Socrates and Alcibiades in the *Symposium* reveals a strong link with the tradition of grounding the text in the authority of credible literary figures. In fact, his attack on the excesses of another Medieval practice—the attribution of allegorical interpretations to classical texts—provides an opportunity for creating an inventory of luminaries ranging from the stoic Cornutus to Ovid, with a brief and unflattering reference to the Florentine humanist Politian. As Gérard Defaux has pointed out, the Medieval legendary figures of the *Pantagruel* prologue have been replaced by the *auctores* favored by the humanists: Homer, Plato, and Horace.[17] The strategy of imbedding the name of a celebrated authority in the *incipit* of the prologue continues in the *Tiers Livre* with the figure of Diogenes the cynic.

The practice is intimately associated with the issue of appropriation, and is not merely a question of dropping names to please and persuade the humanists among his readers. The prologue is structured around the *auctor* highlighted in the *incipit*. Through his narrator M. Alcofrybas, Rabelais appropriates the image of Socrates and the Silenus box in *Gargantua* as well as that of Diogenes and his barrel in the *Tiers Livre* to create a metaphor for his own writing. In spite of the rather folk quality of some of the titles for which he takes credit: *Gargantua, Pantagruel, Fessepinte, La Dignité des Braguettes, Des Poys au lard cum commento,* M. Alcofrybas invites us not to stop at the frivolous appearance of his work, and to proceed from there to the higher meaning, "ains à plus hault sens interpreter ce que par adventure cuidiez dict en gayeté de cueur" (*Gargantua:* p. 7) [but may interpret in a more sublime sense what you may possibly have thought, at first, was uttered in mere light-heartedness] (*Gargantua & Pantagruel:* p. 38).

In the *Tiers Livre* prologue (pp. 393–403), whose heading "Prologue de l'autheur, M. François Rabelais" encourages the reader to equate the narrator with the author, the posture of Diogenes is appropriated by the narrator. His "Je pareillement" [In the same way . . . I] following as it does the long enumeration of Diogenes and his barrel rolling, drives home the metaphor of appropriation. Diogenes and Rabelais—the third person character [*il*] and the first person narrator [*je*]—have a single response to the threat to the city. By rolling his barrel and allowing his fellow countrymen to drink from time to time, he hopes to refresh them and to prove himself useful. The author's objectives set forth in the prologue conform completely to both Cicero's expressed goals for the exordium and to Horace's notion that poetry should please and instruct.[18]

The Quart Livre (the prologue of the 1552 edition) opens with the same active, personal appeal to readers, generalized to good people ["gens de bien"], and continues to instruct and entertain by means of the skillful intermingling of example, commentary, and a full-blown tale to be discussed in a later chapter of this study. The narrator mixes such prominent classical authorities as Galen and Aesop with his contemporary André Tiraqueau "le bon, le docte, le saige, le tant humain, tant debonnaire et equitable," (*Le Quart Livre:* p. 13); [the good, the learned, the wise, the most humane, most noble and most just] (*Gargantua & Pantagruel:* p. 440). Although the authoritative figures give way to the animated story of Couillatris, the juxtaposition of ancient and modern *auctores* reminds the reader that authority is not merely a question of Antiquity but of utility and service to the social order in any period.

Rabelais's contemporary, Bonaventure Des Périers, begins the prologue to the *Nouvelles Récréations et Joyeux Devis* with no reference to the *auctores*. The narrator's first person is secure in engaging the reader in conversation and in explaining the circumstances of the publication of the work. When he does mention Plato and Xenophon later on in the prologue, it is to contradict them or to put their authority in question—in this case, concerning their portrayal of Socrates as austere and cool tempered (*Nouvelles Récréations:* pp. 17–18). Here, the *je* of the narrator and the *il* of the *auctor* do not fuse as in Rabelais's appropriation of Diogenes, but instead, the narrative *je* sets itself apart from the authority: "il n'y a ne Platon, ne Xenophon, qui le me fist accroyre" [neither Plato nor Xenophon has convinced me of it]. It is possible to challenge written authority even from the vulnerable position of the liminary text.

Des Périers appears to be conscious of carving out for himself a new means of literary production. This is clear in the way he talks about his decision not to wait until peace comes but, instead, to publish immediately: "j'ay mieux aimé *m'avancer,* pour vous donner moyen de tromper le temps, meslant des resjouissances parmy vos fascheries" [I preferred to *go ahead* and give you a way to while away the time by mixing merriment with your troubles] (italics mine). We remember that Weimann had contrasted the Middle Ages, where "the means and modes of the author's discourse were not so much the result of his own 'labor,'" with the Renaissance, "where the rise of literary property went hand in hand with new sets of rules about property in the production and reception of fictional discourse."[19] Marking his departure from traditional patterns of appropriation, anchored in the association of the work in progress with the *auctores* of the past, Des Périers takes credit for his innovation, highlighted by the signifier "m'avancer." Instead of waiting, he ventures forward— not in the tracks of Socrates or Diogenes—but in unexplored territory.

However innovative his narrative voice, the structure of Des Périers's preamble carries certain traces of the academic and literary prologues of the Middle Ages. First, it is structured around the seven generating circumstances of the text, a device used frequently in the Medieval period: for whom? [vous/you], what? [les nouvelles/tales], why? [tromper le temps/while away the time'], in what manner? [resjouir/to make merry'], where/when? [icy le vrai temps/here the right time], whence? [j'ayme mieux les prendre pres/I prefer to find them close at hand].[20] Although the narrator neglects the *auctores*, he retains the Medieval practice of including a *sententia:* "Le plus gentil enseignement pour le vie, c'est *Bene vivere et laetari*" [The greatest lesson for living is to live well and rejoice] (*Nouvelles Récréations:* p. 14), interpreted by Lionello Sozzi as knowing how to laugh at one's weakness and learning to be one's own judge (*Nouvelles Récréations:* p. 14).[21] His maxim becomes a *leit motif* for the prologue and culminates in the anecdote concerning Plaisantin, who carries humor and laughter to his deathbed. Although the narration does not begin with the *sententia,* much of the preamble is in fact a *glose* of the *bene vivere et laetari* maxim.[22]

In spite of these reminders of the Medieval prologue, we witness the emergence of a more subjective literary voice in Des Périers's *Préambule* and for which he claims proprietary rights. It is, in fact, the narrator who creates the analogy between *nouvelles* and *marchandises:* "Sinon que vous me vueillez dire que les nouvelles ne sont pas comme les marchandises: et qu'on les donne pour le pris qu'elles coustent" [Unless you wish to tell me that tales are not like merchandise and that they are up for sale for the cost of production] (*Nouvelles Récréations:* p. 16). Unlike his predecessors who sought novelty in the exotic, he will choose his tales from the local repertoire of anecdotes: "j'ayme mieulx les prendre pres" [I prefer to gather them close by]. He is at once making claims for the originality of his text and setting new ground rules for the production of his tales.

While Rabelais only leaves the monuments of past literary history behind in the final paragraph of his prologues, when instructing his chosen readership and insulting the hostile public, Des Périers's preamble is dominated by the present tense and the imperative mode. Guiding the future reception of the text takes precedence over the evocation of past literary giants.

By imbedding the name of a single illustrious precursor, Boccaccio, at a critical place in the prologue to the *Heptaméron*, Marguerite situates the work securely in the short narrative tradition shared by Italy and France. The narrator's reference to Boccaccio three times at the end of the text is just the culmination of a gradual process of allusion to the model, the *Decameron*. Similarities in the circumstances: a disaster, the ladies accompanied by their gentlemen *serviteurs*, Parlamente's telling blush just before the reference to Boccaccio, all bring to mind the textual source. By the time Parlamente utters the name of the source: "je croy qu'il n'y a nulle de vous qui n'ait leu les cent Nouvelles de Bocace" [I don't think there's one of you who hasn't read the hundred tales by Boccaccio] the reader is already reflecting on parallels between the two texts.[23] Laurent Jenny aptly describes the play of the intertextual reference as an allusion which is enough to introduce into the main text a meaning, a story, or even an ideological concept without necessarily explicitly mentioning these elements in detail.[24] Marguerite strengthens the authority of her text by coupling Boccaccio's name with the endorsement of his work by the French royal family:

> . . . les cent Nouvelles de Bocace, nouvellement traduictes d'ytalien en françois, que le roy François, premier de son nom, monseigneur le Daulphin, madame la Daulphine, madame Marguerite, font tant de cas, que si Bocace . . . les eut peu oyr, il debvoit resusciter à la louange de telles personnes.[25] (*L'Heptaméron:* p. 9)

> [. . . the one hundred tales by Boccacio, which have been newly translated from Italian into French, and which are so highly thought of by the King Francis, first, of this name, by Monseigneur the Dauphin, Madame the

Dauphine, and Madame Marguerite. If Boccaccio could have heard them, he would have come back to life on hearing the praise of such great people.]

We see the chain of authority pass from the "texte d'origine" to the king and then to Marguerite herself, mentioned above. What better way to legitimize her literary enterprise than to give it royal approval at the outset?

Marguerite's strategy of self appropriation through self inscription is played down in the Prologue because of the extreme discretion of the narrator and the reluctance to use the first person. There is no explicit textual identity between the narrator and "madame Marguerite," the historical figure referred to in a remote third person. The lack of a *prooemium*, such as we find in the *Decameron* and in which the author justifies his undertaking, further discourages such an equation between narrator and the historical figure of the author inscribed in the prologue.

In Noël du Fail's *Propos rustiques*, no steps are taken to discourage the identification of the narrator with the author, whose name is transparently veiled in the anagram Leon Ladulfi. The first person [*je/I*] of the prologue, addressed by Leon Ladulfi to the "amy lecteur" [reader/friend], flows into the *je/I* of the first chapter with no apparent rupture in identity. The author sets in place two strategies for the authorization of the text. The first involves the appropriation of a rhetorical device in which one term, *rustique*, is explained by its opposite, *noble* or *noblesse*. Discoursing on the origin of class distinction, he goes on to cite the value and "nobility" of rural life, and grounds his examples in the authority of the great Greek and Latin *auctores*: Plato, Virgil, and Horace. He cites the valiant men who left the honest professions of wine production and agriculture to assume the role of statesmen, including Cincinnatus.[26]

Secondly, not satisifed with basing the authority of his text on the testimony ["tesmoignage"] of classical authors, Ladulfi/Du Fail inscribes himself in the initial chapter of his work as eye witness and scribe to what is to follow. Self inscription leads to self authorization; the pure truth ["pure vérité"] of the village elders will reveal itself thanks to their plain (i.e. noble) speech unadorned by rhetorical colors and his own hard labor ["bonne besogne"]. The courageous image of the good plowman ["bon laboureur"] developed in the preface becomes a metaphor for his own writing efforts, as he ends the initial chapter by comparing himself to the carter pushing against a heavily-laden cart:

> ... et mestoit une telle peine que au charretier qui, pour ayder à ses chevaux atteilez à la charrette trop chargee, met son chappeau entre son espaule et la roue, pour aucunement les soulager, aucunesfois beuvant à son baril, attaché au collier du cheval de devant. (*Propos rustiques:* p. 608)
>
> [... and put out such an effort as a carter might who, to help his horses harnessed to an overloaded wagon, puts his hat between his shoulder and the wheel to ease their toil a bit, and drinking now and then from his cask, attached to the collar of the horse in front.]

The metaphor of the carter embodies the objectives of the prologuist in guiding the work along but letting the characters speak for themselves. In this strategy of self inscription as an eyewitness to the events and conversation related in the prologue, we see two important links with the past: first, with the theatrical prologues of ancient Greece, where the prologue "in the form of a narrative was designed to familiarize the audience with the myth that was a subject of the tragedy and with the circumstances of the action;" second, with the preambles of the *chansons de geste*, which often evoked the testimony of eye witnesses.[27] The first chapter serves to introduce both the players of Du Fail's work and the prologuist as key witness. As Ladulfi walks up to the village elders and lends an ear to their remarks, he reminds us that wisdom comes from age and experience as well as from books and formal education. Instead of the *translatio studii* carried out by the medieval authors of classically inspired romances, Ladulfi sets out to transmit the common sense wisdom of his neighboring villagers.[28] Downplaying his own contribution in order to highlight the narrative gift of his country neighbors, the *préfacier* assumes a respectful posture. He defers personal appropriation in the interest of giving due credit to his source—not the authoritative sources of antiquity but, like Des Périers, the sources close at hand—the wisdom of his own region.

For quite different reasons, appropriation assumes a central role in the Louise Labé's *Débat de Folie et d'Amour*. In the prefatory epistle addressed to Clémence de Bourges, appropriation concerns not only personal honor but the glorification of a muted sector of society—women.[29] Study and self-expression is an obligation to women so recently granted access to science and letters. Women's success in studying and writing will give lasting proof of the ills perpetuated by men for so long barring their female counterparts from the intellectual world. Labé perceives what Hélène Cixous discusses centuries later, namely, that writing is the very possibility of change ["l'écriture est la possibilité même du changement"].[30] In appropriating for herself that which cannot be stolen from her—in contrast to the usual embellishments of the female sex such as chains, rings, and sumptuous clothes [chaines, anneaux et somptueus habits]—she will achieve a degree of long lasting, inviolable honor: "Mais l'honneur que la science nous procurera, sera entierement notre: et ne nous pourra estre ôté" (*Débat*, 17, ll. 13–15); [But the honor which knowledge will bring us will be entirely our own and cannot be taken from us,] (translation mine). Here, Labé uses the inclusive pronoun *nous* to embrace all women given to putting their thoughts to writing [concepcions par escrit].

Assessing her own efforts and limitations, Labé stresses that it is the reputation of the muted sex which is at stake:

"Et outre la reputacion que notre sexe en recevra, nous aurons valu au publiq, que les hommes mettront plus de peine et d'estude aus sciences vertueuses, de peur qu'ils ayent honte de voir proceder celes, desquelles ils ont pretendu estre tousjours superieurs quasi en tout." (*Débat*, 18, ll. 33–38)

[And in addition to the recognition that our sex will gain by this, we will have furnished the public with a reason for men to devote more study and labor to the humanities lest they might be ashamed to see us surpass them when they have always pretended to be superior in nearly everything.] ("Louise Labé": p. 149)

Women who give themselves to letters can both contribute to the honor of their sex and serve as an inspiration for those who had previously excluded them from learning. The author suggests an ironic reversal of roles with significant implications for the furthering of *belles-lettres*.

Up to this point in the prefatory epistle, we seem to be dealing with a straightforward call to women to give themselves to study and to surpass or equal men in knowledge and virtue [en science et vertu passer ou égaler les hommes] (*Débat*, 18, ll. 25–26). The appropriation of learning by and for women is central to Labé's appeal. Her appeal is personal, not couched in authoritative sources. Yet, in the midst of her appeal, appears a curious echo of an authoritative text:

> je ne puis faire autre chose que prier les vertueuses Dames d'eslever un peu leurs esprits par dessus leurs quenoilles et fuseaus, et s'employer à faire entendre au monde que si nous ne sommes faites pour commander, si ne devons nous estre desdaignées pour compagnes tant es afaires domestiques que publiques, de ceus qui gouvernent et se font obeïr. (*Débat*, 18, ll. 26-33)

> [I cannot do otherwise than beg excellent Ladies to raise their minds a little above their distaffs and spindles and to exert themselves to make it clear to the world that, if we are not made to command, we ought not to be disdained as companions in both domestic and public affairs by those who govern and command obedience.] ("Louise Labé": p. 149)

It is not simply the allusion to distaffs and spindles which brings to mind the *proemio* to Boccaccio's *Decameron,* but what Michael Riffaterre refers to as an ungrammaticality in the adaptation of the intertext.[31] Boccaccio as prologuist writes to offer support, help, and refuge to those women who love [quelle che amano]. For other women, the needle, spindle and wool winder offer sufficient diversion [per ciò che all'altre è assai l'ago e 'l fuso e l'arcolaio].[32] In Labé's image, the woman, not the man, is the productive scholar and writer, while the man is a passive witness to her creative activity, and will in turn be inspired by her example. Boccaccio, we remember, wrote for women because they were cooped up and had no outlet for their sorrows, while men could find distraction in hunting, fishing, riding and other outdoor activities. Such constraints on woman's freedom to choose her own pastimes is precisely what Labé refers to as the "severes loix des hommes" [harsh laws of men] at the outset of her prefatory epistle. Yet the activities cited by Boccaccio are the pastimes of nobles—physical activities. Louise's ladies will use their newfound freedom to exercise the mind not the body: "pour aquerir cet honneur que les lettres et sciences ont acoutumé porter aus personnes qui les suyvent" (*Débat*, 18, ll. 42-44); [to acquire that honor which literature and the sciences are accustomed to bring the persons who follow them] ("Louise Labé": p. 149).

Her dialogue with the authoritative text and author continues as she argues that the pleasures of the senses—the subject of both the *Decameron* and her own book—pass quickly. Recording our thoughts provides a double pleasure, for we can not only relive a pleasurable moment but reflect on our state of mind at the moment the pleasure was experienced.

Even while generating a text that seeks to appropriate discursive practices for and by women, Labé implicitly engages a formidable *auctor* in a dialogue which might go unperceived without the play of the intertext. By appropriating the spinning motif or hypogram from Boccaccio and reversing key elements, she convincingly argues the case for woman's place as intellectual role model.[33] The demonstrated authority of the intertext only strengthens the weight of her argument. The prefatory epistle of Labé's *Débat* offers an example of the strategy of authorization working to facilitate the appropriation of discourse by women.

Neither Noël du Fail nor Louise Labé confesses to writing exclusively for personal motives. Labé purports to write in part to hold up her own in the fight for woman's equality, while Du Fail records the everyday wisdom of the village elders in a more permanent form than their oral exchanges permit.

If there is a common link between Noël du Fail and Michel de Montaigne, it is to be found not in a comparison of their two prologues—both addressed "Au lecteur" [To the Reader]—but rather in a comparison of the first chapter of the *Propos rustiques* to Montaigne's notice to the reader. We could trace a line following the emergence of literary subjectivity stretching from the conversational prologue of Des Périers's *Nouvelles Récréations*, passing through the first chapter of the *Propos rustiques,* and continuing in Montaigne's preliminary remarks to his reader.

We are dealing with authors who are plainly cognizant of the choices they face: "alternative modes of production in terms of language, style, models, and audience."[34] By speaking in a simple, natural style, the narrator/author seeks to impose his presence on the reader. In the *Propos rustiques*, no equivalency has yet been established between the *I* of the narrator and the book. The credit for production is shared by the author and the village elders. In the *Essais*, the *I* who generates the text and the product are one creative force. Montaigne's "Au lecteur" is a total act of appropriation: "Ainsi, lecteur, je suis moymesmes la matière de mon livre" [Thus, reader, I am myself the matter of my book.][35] Authority for the book lies solely with the *I* who introduces himself in the prologue. Here is an author who is fully aware of the "property status" of his work and who claims initially that it does not belong to the general public, but to his friends and relatives: "à la commodité particulière de mes parens et amis" [to the private convenience of my relatives and friends] (*"Au lecteur," Essais*, 9; 2).[36]

What Montaigne seems to be claiming is not so much paternity for his work as identity with it.[37] Montaigne aims at recreating his portrait as an exact replica—not life like but the life itself—a process which Barry Lydgate calls not *mimetic* but *incarnational*:[38] "Je veus qu'on m'y voie en ma façon simple, naturelle et ordinaire, sans contantion et artifice: car c'est moy que je peins" [I want to be seen here in my simple, natural, ordinary fashion, without straining or artifice, for it is myself that I portray] ("Au lecteur," *Essais*, 9; 2). The speaker's insistence on the first person and on its representation in the work excludes the *auctores* from the liminary text and underscores the personal and unique nature of his writing.

Montaigne eventually sets his "moy," portrayed in its entirety, against the fragmented self advanced by established "autheurs":[39]

> Les autheurs se communiquent au peuple par quelque marque particuliere et estrangere; moy, le premier, par mon estre universel, comme Michel de Montaigne, non comme grammarien, ou poëte ou jurisconsulte. (III, ii. 782c)

> [Authors communicate with the people by some special extrinsic mark; I am the first to do so by my entire being, as Michel de Montaigne, not as a grammarian or a poet or a jurist.] (III, ii, 611c)

Only in the third book is he able to explain his ambivalent attitude toward the *auctores*, whom he at once admires and fears—fears because their style might invade his own and destroy its natural integrity: "Quand j'escris, je me passe bien de la compagnie et souvenance des livres, de peur qu'ils n'interrompent ma forme" [When I write, I prefer to do it without the company and remembrance of books, for fear they may interfere with my style] (III, v, 852b; 666b).[40]

With Montaigne and his "Au lecteur," the Medieval concept of the *Livre*—the sum of all sources making up a firmly authorized literary tradition—gives way to *mon livre*: "Ainsi, lecteur, je suis moy-mesmes la matiere de mon livre" [Thus reader, I am myself the matter of my book] ("Au lecteur," *Essais*, 8; 2). The process of personal authorization of the text, begun with Des Périers, has been completed, and the act of appropriation is signed and sealed when the first person possessive adjective is attached to the word book. Only the humility formula, used as the author protests his unworthiness, and the oath of veracity remind us of the Medieval prologue and its classical origins.[41]

2

Nue vérité ou invention poétique?
History and Fiction in the Prologue of the Renaissance *Nouvelle*

Setting the text within the appropriate literary tradition through the mention of worthy precursors is not the only task of the prologue. It marks the threshold separating the historical, material world of the author from the fictional world of the text. No matter how far removed the author's fiction may be from reality as perceived by the sixteenth century mind, the prologue inevitably situates itself in relation to the historic period in which the text was conceived. When Parlamente, in the Prologue to the *Heptaméron*, seeks approval for her project to follow Boccaccio's lead in telling stories to lift the spirits of the stranded travellers, she hastens to mention the impact of the *Decameron* on Francis I and the other members of the Royal Family.[1] Such specific reference to the literary taste of the King's immediate family and to the Dauphin's dislike of rhetorical embellishment keeps the reader suspended between the fictional cadre of the flood unfolding on the printed page and the referential reality behind the story—the court of Francis I so closely associated with the author Marguerite de Navarre.

Discussing the development of the *nouvelle* in the late Middle Ages, Roger Dubuis remarks on the narrator's need to authenticate the events in the narrative. In the *Cent Nouvelles Nouvelles*, it was often done through the occasional and often unexpected appearance of historic personalities in the midst of a fictional account of the type we find in Marguerite's Prologue, composed almost eighty years after the *Cent Nouvelles Nouvelles*. Dubuis describes the unexpected appearance of a figure from history as a passing silhouette which gives the illusion of truth.[2] Why then this need to authenticate an obviously fictive narrative with historical allusions? To what extent was this tradition carried on in the prologues of Renaissance *conteurs*? Medieval treatises tend to play down the role of *inventio* in rhetoric, no doubt because, as William Nelson reminds us, "the imagination itself was distrusted as the faculty which distorted and falsified reality."[3] Fabri's *Le Grand et Vray Art de pleine rhétorique* contains just a brief discussion under the heading of *De Invention* in contrast to the more detailed treatment of the other parts of rhetoric. And yet, since the classical rhetoricians placed invention as the first or principal object of rhetoric—a classification retained by Fabri—scholars of rhetoric could not ignore it.[4]

We know that the Medieval distrust of poetic invention carries over into the Renaissance, as is revealed in Jacques Amyot's Prologue to his translation of Plutarch's *Parallel Lives*. Historic examples based on naked truth ["nue verité"], he tells us, are more effective than fabrications and poetic compositions ["les inventions et compositions poëtiques"] because they not only illustrate heroic action but give us the desire to act courageously. Invention, whose goal is to delight, leads to exaggeration, while history instructs in its attention to honest detail.[5] The authors of the Renaissance understood the term *inventio* in its classical sense as the generation of propositions or arguments. In suggesting the fictional underpinnings of *invention*, Amyot endows the word with the meaning it will take on in the modern era.

Yet history, for Amyot, is clearly linked to the narrative tradition. It is "une narration ordonnee des choses notables, *dictes, faictes* ou advenues par le passé pour en conserver la souvenance à perpetuité, et en servir d'instruction à la posterité" [an orderly narration of notable things, *uttered, accomplished*, or come about in the past, for the purpose of preserving their memory and serving as instruction for future generations] (*Vies*, iii v°, emphasis added). History is not merely the noteworthy event that took place, but the retelling of the event for posterity. We are not far from the Medieval concept of the *estoire*—the source worthy of belief. History is the collective memory of human life, a treasury preserving the memorable words and deeds of mankind. Nor is history dependent on the written word. Amyot cites the transmission of historic events in epic songs in the past but also in stories told by barbarians dwelling in newly discovered lands ["barbares habitans és terres neufves" in his own time] (*Vies*, iii v°). History and poetic composition share form and order imposed by the act of narration. Amyot distinguishes one from the other by the fact that history is based on the actual words and deeds of meritorious people. Poetic invention can delight but does not have sufficient weight to instruct and inspire to noble action.

That Amyot should defend history against poetic invention is understandable in a work devoted to the scrupulous depiction of illustrious figures of Antiquity. More puzzling is the significant role given to historic reference in the prologues of short narrative form whose art depends on the author's ability to embellish what would otherwise remain an anecdote drawn from literary sources or from contemporary life. One explanation can be directly linked to the short narrative genre itself. In addressing his work to the Duke of Burgundy, the author of the *Cent Nouvelles Nouvelles* comments on the innovative nature of his work. In contrast to Boccaccio's *Cent Nouvelles*, his own tales are of quite recent date ["d'assez fresche memoire"] and have a new look ["de myne beaucoup nouvelles"]. The dedication invites us to interpret *nouvelle* in terms of chronology—the recent past—and in terms of qualitative innovation—the new look, something not yet seen, in short, as Dubuis points out, ["inédite"] or disseminated for the first time.[6] The *nouvelle* as genre is intimately associated with the *nouvelle* as newsworthy event, and such an association leads the prologuist to view the narrative event in terms of recent if not contemporary history.

For those storytellers who wrote *nouvelles*, there were expectations that the narrative would in some respect reflect recent if not current events. Yet we know that some of the tales were drawn from literary sources and date back to the Middle Ages. As writers begin to take liberties with the geographic region or the chronological period in which the tale is set, they become a part of the play of fiction. Hayden White tells us that both historical and fictional narratives must "stand the test of coherence and plausibility".[7] Fiction is in fact sometimes more plausible than actual events. Instead of admitting the role invention plays in their writing, storytellers turn to the tricks of the chroniclers—oaths of veracity, eyewitness accounts by reputable people—and then proceed to spin their tales.[8] A kind of duplicity evolves between the narrator and the reader in which both recognize that the narrative is not to be confused with "true history."[9] Only when this pact has been agreed upon can the tale achieve its goal of delighting and instructing.[10]

Let us turn to specific prologues of the Renaissance *conteurs* to see how they involve the reader in a duplicitous pact where fiction becomes history in the interest of entertainment and moral improvement—explicit goals repeated again and again in the prologues to collections of tales. One might expect that Philippe de Vigneulles, better known for his historical works of Metz and Lorraine, would feel obliged to situate the generating circumstances of his *Cent Nouvelles Nouvelles* (1515) in time and space. Although the beginning of the prologue has been lost, what remains starts mid-sentence with specific reference to the two kings of France who reigned when his own literary model, the anonymous *Cent Nouvelles Nouvelles*, was first written and then flourished: Charles VII and Louis XI. For this historian, it is clear that history and events beget narration and invention. The truces ["treves"] between battles gave the gentlemen soldiers the leisure time to recount stories. The role of the author is limited to gathering and recording the stories which had first circulated orally: "Lesquelles histoires ung vaillant acteur en ait recueillez cent et en ait faict et composé ung livre lequel se nomme, et l'a intitulé, les *Cent Nouvelles Nouvelles*" [A valiant author has gathered one hundred of these stories and conceived and put together a book which is called and bears the title *One Hundred New Tales*].[11] *Inventio* is clearly not advanced as the first task of the author, who in the above passage seems more concerned with *dispositio* and *elocutio* in his task of transcribing the tales. Classical rhetoric subordinates these last two elements to invention.[12]

Specific self reference—"moy Phelippe de Vigneulle, marchans de drap et simple d'entendement" [I, Philippe de Vigneulles, cloth merchant and man of simple understanding]—serves the purpose of rescuing the first *Cent Nouvelles Nouvelles* and its valiant author from attacks by the simple people ["simple gens"] who doubt its veracity. Our historian/cloth merchant begins to stretch his definition of truth from the historically documented event to that which *could* occur— that which is plausible: "à quoy je respons et dis qu'on peut croire que possible est esté advenus. Et peut on croire toutes choses qui ne sont contraires à Dieu ne à sa loy" [to which I answer and say that one can believe that it is possible that it happened. And one can believe all things that do not run contrary to God or to his law] (Vigneulles, 57). Vigneulles justifies invention as long as the reader retains the good and avoids the evil.

It is through his attention to historic detail: his illness "en l'an cinqz cens et cinqz" [in the year 1505], along with his personal testimony to the authenticity of the tales occurring in Metz or nearby, that Philippe convinces the reader to accept his creative efforts. Philippe's posture as a man of simple intellectual powers—"mon ygnorance et mon simple entendement" [my ignorance and simple understanding]—only reinforces the reader's conviction that he will be straightforward, truthful, and to the point.[13] Cicero reminds us, after all, that clarity is another quality of eloquence, and by extension, of rhetorical play.[14] Philippe imbeds his motive for writing in a series of disclaimers about his literary shortcomings—the *excusatio propter infirmitatem* topos of which Gérard Genette speaks in his recent work on the functions of the prologue.[15] Vigneulles's narrator asks us to view his book of tales as living proof that specific local incidents ["adventures"], compiled by a competent narrator ["bon facteur"], make excellent literary material.[16] Fiction's best source can be found in the historic events unfolding within our own cities and towns—the *hic et nunc* as opposed to the remote past and exotic settings of certain medieval narrative genres.[17]

In a curious twist, oral transmission ("ouy dire" or hearsay) between creditable citizens lends historic authenticity to a tale and gives proof that the incident is in fact new and newsworthy ["d'assez fresche memoire"]. Philippe hastens to mention in his prologue that he has either witnessed the events recounted in his book or heard them recounted: "du moins je les ouy dire et racompter à gens digne de foy et de creance" [or at least heard them recounted by people worthy of faith and belief]. Nicolas de Troyes admits to having borrowed some tales for his *Grand Parangon des Nouvelles Nouvelles* from written sources; "les autres j'ay ouy racompter à plusieurs bons compaignons et d'aulcunes que j'ay veu faire en mon absence et à moy mesmes" [the others I have heard recounted to several good friends and some I've known to have gone on in my absence or even some have happened to me] (p. 5).[18] Hearsay lends plausibility to the account, for people "digne de foy" would not waste their time listening attentively to idle gossip.

It is tempting to see in the preamble to Des Périers *Nouvelles Récréations et Joyeux Devis* a continuation of the concept of short narrative form grounded firmly in history. As Vigneulles had done, Des Périers begins by alluding to an historic event—the long awaited peace between Francis I and Charles V. Whereas Vigneulles had specifically named the monarchs in question, Des Périers leaves the reader to guess to which peace or truce he is referring: "Je vous gardoys ce joyeux propos à quand la paix seroit faicte" [I was keeping these joyous words for after peace was made].[19] His invitation challenges attentive readers to speculate on the exact date of composition; many have answered the challenge, but as Krystyna Kasprzyk points out, the allusion is vague.[20] What begins as seemingly well-grounded in a specific historic event gives way rapidly to indifference to historic specificity. Time is relative; we have little control over war and peace, sickness and health. Laughter is appropriate at all times and is a good remedy for sorrow: "Ne vault il pas mieux se resjouir, en attendant mieux: que se fascher d'une chose qui n'est pas en nostre puissance" [Isn't it better to rejoice while waiting for better times than to get upset over things beyond our control?] (*Nouvelles Récréations:* p. 14).[21] The narrator's and the reader's frame of reference is the present of discourse.[22] That which is no longer present—failed peace initiative—and that which is going to be present—the long awaited and uncertain peace—lie largely beyond our control and merit no more textual attention then the brief mention at the outset of the preamble.

After playing with historic context, Des Périers rejects all notion of second-level meanings: "il n'y ha point de sens allegoricque, mistique, fantastique" [there are no allegorical, mystical, or fantastic meanings' (*Nouvelles Récréations:* p. 15). He cautions us against looking for the historic identity of the players or the setting: "Riez seulement, et ne vous chaille si ce fut Gaultier ou si ce fut Garguille. Ne vous souciez point si ce fut à Tours en Berry ou à Bourges en Touraine" [Just laugh, and don't worry if it was Gaultier or if it was Garguille. Don't worry if it happened in Tours in Berry or in Bourges in Touraine]. In contrast to Vigneulles, who stresses the oral transmission of the tales at a distinct moment in the past, Des Périers highlights the present of the reading experience and the pleasure derived from it: "Ouvrez le livre: si ung compte ne vous plait, hay à l'aultre" [Open the book; if a tale doesn't please you, select another one] (*Nouvelles Récréations:* p. 15); "Riez si vous voulez. . . .Lisez hardiment, dames et demoyselles : il n'y a rien qui ne soit honneste" [Laugh if you wish. . . . Read boldly on, ladies and young ladies: there is nothing that is not proper] (p. 17). Entertainment is the goal of fiction, and the search for historic accuracy is left to members of the legal profession (contract specialists *faiseurs de contractz* and litigators *intenteurs de proces:* p. 15). But Des Périers joins Vigneulles in giving preference to local source material for his tales. Recent material, like goods, has a fresher appeal. Exotic settings or unfamiliar customs can only impede the pleasurable experience derived from reading or hearing a *nouvelle*, whose success depends upon an unexpected twist at the end.[23]

Narrators who set for themselves the task of writing down tales told orally are more likely to stress the historic accuracy of their transcription. In the address from the prologuist Leon Ladulfi—anagram for Noël du Fail—to his reader, the narrator laments the fact that historians largely sang the praises of their patrons, the upper classes, and so the "noblesse" of the peasants has gone unsung. In the guise of witness turned historian, Ladulfi pledges to record their conversations, not in the high style ["style eslevé"] but in a style suited to the humble nature of their topics: "pource que à tel sainct telle offrande, tel mercier, tel panier" [for let the offering suit the saint, the habberdasher the basket].[24] Accuracy in reporting comes in the form of strict respect for the tone of their conversations and in the attention paid to physical details of dress, gesture, and personality of the village elders. There is scant concern for either historic or geographic details in the opening frame; the events are shrouded in imprecision: sometimes ["quelquefois"], on a holiday ["à jour de feste"], two or three holidays ["deux ou trois festes"], nearby villages ["villages prochains"] (*Propos rustiques:* pp. 607–8). The artist's efforts are devoted to painting an accurate and sympathetic picture of rural life: the people, their customs, and their interests. *Enargeia*, or "the evocation of the visual scene in all its details and colors, as if the reader were present," is more effective in winning our affection for his villagers than the amassing of events and details.[25]

More than twenty years later, Jacques Yver's narrator of *Le Printemps* appears more comfortable in the role of *chroniqueur*. His confidence grows out of his belief that witnesses in a court case need not be eloquent as long as the deposition is true and certain ["vraie et certaine"]. Like Ladulfi, he assumes the role of faithful secretary, and with a great deal more attention to historic detail, recounts the generating circumstances of his narrative. The illustrious band of gentlemen and young ladies ["illustre compagnie de gentilhommes et demoiselles"] meets at Pentecost as a remedy for the sorrow they have suffered during the religious wars: "afin de soulager par aimiable fréquentation les ennuis reçus durant cette misérable guerre civile" [to relieve with pleasant company the troubles suffered during this wretched civil war].[26] The fiction of his story vies for textual prominence with the chronicle of the religious wars. Metaphors of nature—the calm after the storm, the lively chirping of the birds after a long winter—evoke the feeling of the people of France at the outset of peace. Specific historic dating is made possible through the metaphor of bloodletting. Reference to the third "saignée" [bloodletting] which has brought relief to France's wretched, weakened body ["ce pauvre corps attenué"] allows us to date the preface from the end of the third religious war (1568–1570), marked by the Peace of Saint-Germain in 1570. The storyteller turned chronicler narrows the focus to the people of Poitou, where his story will take place:

> je peux bien assurer que entre tous les François, les habitants du pays de Poitou retournèrent avec extreme joie en leurs désolées maisons, pensant entrer en nouveaux ménages, où ils réputoient pour gagné ce qu'ils trouvoient de reste et qui étoit échappé aux insolents soldats. (*Le Printemps:* p. 522)

> [I can give assurance that among all the French people, the inhabitants of the Poitou region returned to their abandoned houses with extreme joy, intending to set up house again, where they considered well earned whatever they found that remained and that had escaped the insolent soldiers.]

Here is a narrator as absorbed by the recent events of his country as by the narrative frame he is describing. Yver's debt to the *Decameron* lies in his making the frame story emerge from a recent civil crisis. Like Boccaccio's narrator, the narrator of *Le Printemps* assumes the roles of chronicler and *conteur* with equal fervor. Story and history are inextricably interwoven.

Once the time and the place have been established, the narrator shies away from naming the participants in the elegant proceedings but instead clothes their identity in allegorical names reminiscent of medieval romances: "les sieurs de Bel-Accueil, de Fleur d'Amour et de Ferme-Foi" [(Lords) of Fair Welcome, Flower of Love, and Firm Faith.] The narrator claims, paradoxically, that fictitious names permit the personality of his characters to appear. The discovery of the historical identity of the players turns our attention away from their assumed roles in the narrative:

> J'ay délibéré de faire comme ceux qui jouent sur le théatre : lesquels sous des masques empruntés représentent les vrais personnages . . . et moi, sous ces noms feints, je représenterai la verité. (*Le Printemps:* p. 522)

> [I thought to do as those who act on stage, who beneath borrowed masks play true characters . . . and I, under these false names, will represent the truth.]

The theater image placed at the opening of his work helps to explain the importance of giving the illusion of truth within a fictional work. The careful development of narrative action is what creates plausible fiction—independent of specific reference to historic or autobiographical details. As Nancy Regalado explains in her work on Rutebeuf, "the public sought the poet in the work rather than the man behind the poet."[27] Yver clearly understands the difference between history and fiction, and finds room for both in the liminary spece of his work. Yet again, the historic details help convince the reader that the *nouvelles* concern the recent past. History serves the rhetorical aim of winning the goodwill and attention of the public.[28] Something which all of the collections of tales discussed above have in common, with the exception of the *Nouvelles Récréations*, is the narrator's posture as accurate and faithful scribe to a group of *devisants*. Truthsaying figures prominently in the pact they make with their readers. What happens, however, when the contract to transmit historically verifiable material is undermined from the start?

Writing under the pen name Philippe d'Alcripe, Philippe Le Picard pokes fun at the truthsaying convention in the title of his work, *La Nouvelle Fabrique des excellents traicts de verité, livre pour inciter les resveurs tristes et melancholiques à vivre de plaisir* [*The New Work of Truth's Excellent Features, A Book to Incite Sad and Melancholy Dreamers to Live on Pleasure*].[29] The second half of the title characterizes the consumers of tales as dreamers who give primacy to the senses over the intellect. The excellent traits of truth mentioned in the title give way in the prologue, addressed "aux bénévoles lecteurs" [to the kind readers], to the colorful convocation of friends eating and drinking in a tavern in Lyons. The enterprise is grounded in pleasure, not excellence or truth, as evidenced in the choice of vocabulary: "faisant chere lye" [living it up]; "buvantz du meilleur et plus frais" [drinking the best and the coolest]; "maintes joyeuses histoires et plaisans contes" [many merry stories and amusing tales] (*La Nouvelle Fabrique*: p. 9).

History comes into play only as his friends urge him to preserve the stories for their children in the future ["à nos enfans à l'advenir"]. As an afterthought it occurs to Philippe that his work might appeal to another readership—those who worship the truth: "desirant aussi par semblable faire chose aggreable aux amateurs et secteurs de pure verité" [and so wishing in the same way to do something pleasant for the lovers and worshippers of pure truth] (p. 10). Again, his expressed aim is not to incite to virtuous action, but to please, to appeal to the senses ["faire chose aggreable"]. Even truthseekers respond more quickly to that which is pleasurable.

The *préfacier* tells stories to divert and put the mind at ease: "Ains rapatrier et recreer les esprits humains quelques fois agitez des passions melancoliques, me suis ingeré mettre par escript icelles joyeuses histoires, alias excellents traicts de la vérité" [So to bring home human minds, on occasion stirred up with melancholy feelings, and to cheer them up, I set about writing down these merry tales, alias excellent flashes of truth] (*La Nouvelle Fabrique:* p. 10). In a reversal of the title of the work, in which the truth factor took precedence over the pleasure factor, Philippe identifies his tales first as "joyeuses histoires," and only after as "excellents traicts de vérité." He shows little concern for the detractors who would claim that in writing fiction, he is passing off counterfeit money for good. Setting himself in contrast to the great prognosticators such as Brohon and Nostradamus, who claim to speak the truth and then lie, he hopes to hit upon the truth in the midst of his fictional enterprise: "Pourquoy ne puis-je pas (par vostre foy et la mienne) aussi bien dire verité en pensant mentir" [Why can't I (by your faith and mine) just as well tell the truth thinking that I'm lying?] The standards for fiction are simply different from those set for history. Where pleasure is involved, truth loses its currency. Storytelling—like alchemy—has the power to transform the negative into the positive, to convert sorrow and anger into lightness and joy: "divertira chagrin et fascherie en allegresse et joyeuseté" (*La Nouvelle Fabrique:* p. 12).

The opening sentence of Béroalde de Verville's *Le Moyen de Parvenir* parodies the Renaissance insistence on situating the tale in history. Measures of time are listed roughly in descending order, with only *l'hebdomade* appearing out of place:

> Car est il, que ce fut au temps, au siecle, en l'indiction, en l'Aere, en l'Hegire, en l'hebdomade, au lustre, en l'Olympiade, en l'an, au terme, au mois, à la semaine, au jour, à l'heure, à la minute, et iustement à l'instant que, par l'avis et progrèz du Daimon des sphères, les éteufs descheurent de credit, et qu'au lieu d'eux, furent avancées les molles balles, au préjudice de la noble antiquité qui se jouoit si joliment.[30]

> [So it happens that it was in the time, the century, the indiction, the era, the hegira, the hebdomad, the lustrum, the Olympiad, the year, the term, the month, the week, the day, the hour, the minute, and exactly the instant that by the counsel and progression of the Daemon of the spheres,

hard balls fell out of favor and instead of them, soft balls were proposed, to the detriment of noble ancestry which played so gallantly.]

The reader of Renaissance tales was accustomed to such openings as "Au temps du Roy Louis douziesme" [In the time of Louis XII] (*Heptaméron*, Tale 30), "L'année que Madame Marguerite d'Autriche vint à Cambray" [The year that Madame Marguerite of Austria came to Cambrai] (*Heptaméron*, Tale 41), "N'a guiere que au pays de Lorraine" [A short time ago in the region of Lorraine] (Vigneulles, Tale 33), "Au temps de mon pere" [In my father's time] (Vigneulles, Tale 25). Béroalde offers a series of possible openers, and the inclusion of units of time dating back to antiquity—*indiction* [15 years] and *lustre* [5 years]—reinforces the element of play.[31] It is in fact play, and more specifically, *le jeu de paume* or tennis, which is the object of this long enumeration of chronological units. The narrator dates the generating circumstance of his work not to a national cataclysm such as civil war or pestilence but to the introduction of soft balls to replace the harder balls [*éteufs*].

The poet's regret for the innovation leads him to attack a second commonplace of short narrative form—novelty itself. "Confuz soient ces inventeurs de nouveautez, qui gastent la jeunesse, et contre les bonnes coustumes troublent nos jeux!" [Confound these inventors of new things who spoil the youth and, going against all good customs, disrupt our games] (*Le Moyen de Parvenir*: pp. 2–3). His play on two favorite opening devices for the collections of tales prepares the way for the main theme of his work: "se délecter" [to revel]. All of the present troubles: wars, sickness, syphilis can be traced to this unwelcome novelty come to trouble well established playing practices. Many wise men persist in attributing the ills to other causes, but the narrator sticks by his story: "et je vous jure, sans jurer, que tout est vray" [and I swear to you, without swearing, that everything is true] (*Le Moyen de Parvenir*: p. 3).

In the space of two pages, the narrator has playfully called into question the liminary commonplaces of the Renaissance collections of *contes* and has given them new life. It is hard to take his oath of veracity seriously when the likes of Socrates, Alexander, Bodin, Pythagoras, and Rabelais are summoned to the banquet, and yet, in the light of another intertext, Rabelais's *Gargantua*, we may well imagine that Socrates "fit fort bien son devoir de maschoires" [made good work of his jawing duties] (*Le Moyen de Parvenir*: p. 8–9).[32] For the sixteenth century reader (and perhaps the modern), the fictional Socrates, interlocutor at many lively Renaissance symposia, was more alive and appealing than the remote historic figure. Discussing the primacy of the written word in the Renaissance, Michel Foucault has commented that equal credibility was granted the most varied types of literary or historic sources: "Scriptural commentary, commentaries on ancient authors, commentaries on the accounts of travellers, commentaries on legends and fables: none of these forms of discourse is required to justify its claim to be expressing a truth before it is interpreted; all that is required of it is the possibility of talking about it."[33] The Renaissance reader constructed a hybrid image of Socrates based on many types of discourse: the works of Plato as translated by Renaissance humanists, commentaries on the same works, and allusions to Plato in fictional or satiric works.

In the midst of his wildest claim for the *Moyen de Parvenir*—its status as "centre de tous les livres," the book incorporating all books of the past, present, and future—Béroalde's narrative voice denies all parodic intent and claims absolute authenticity: "ne pensez pas que ce soit mocquerie que de ce simpose et souper philosophicque, le plus autentique qui fut jamais" [don't think that it's a mockery, this symposium and philosophical supper, the most authentic that ever was] (*Le Moyen de Parvenir:* p. 22).[34]

To read a book which claims to contain all books and all wisdom is to enter a pact of complicity with the author/narrator. Béroalde's outrageous claim for his work is his manner of unmasking the fictional contract between his narrator and the willing reader—"ces beaux et fidelles esprits" [those fair and faithful spirits] (p. 28). The contract is based on good faith—good faith to approach fiction with the right frame of mind. Reading with an open mind must surely lie at the heart of the "secret" which the narrator promises to reveal to us. As he had said at the opening: "mais qu'est-ce que jouer? c'est se delecter sans penser en mal" [but what is play? It is to enjoy oneself without misgivings] (*Le Moyen de Parvenir:* p. 3). Near the close of his introduction to the dialogues, he bids us to keep away from those who misunderstand the fictional contract: "estrangez vous de ces pifres presomptueux, qui voyans les bonnes personnes desireuses de se calfeutrer le cerveau d'un peu de bonne lecture et profitable, s'en scandalisent" [Stay clear of those presumptuous meddlers who take offense as soon as they see good people eager to fill their brain with a bit of good, worthwhile reading] (*Le Moyen de Parvenir:* p. 27).

The rare secret he promises is not only his book but his approach to reading fiction: "Je m'en rapporte à ces sages et prudens Prestres, qui nomment leur breviaire leur femme" [I rely on those wise and cautious priests who refer to their breviary as their wife.]

The prologuist who calls fiction history is no more at fault than the priest who jokingly calls his prayer book his wife. The metaphors of fiction allow the priest to view his celibate status with good humor. The success of these collections of *nouvelles* is linked to their ambiguous status between historical truth and plausible fiction, and it is the role of the prologue to call attention to the ambiguity without entirely destroying the illusion. The charm of the Renaissance tale depends on the *glissement* between fictional development of character and the silhouetted events and figures of history.

The modern reader needs to bear in mind that history, in the Renaissance, was considered to be a branch of literature—a branch that had an ethical charge to inspire to right action. To achieve this end, the narrative of the historic event had to obey the same aesthetic and rhetorical principles that governed other branches of literature.[35] History and more fanciful forms of narrative were thus inextricably bound by the strategies that served to give shape to the story. In the end, as Montaigne tells us, "les tesmoignages fabuleux, pourveu qu'ils soient possibles, y servent comme les vrais" [fabulous testimonies, provided they are possible, serve like true ones] (I, xxi, 104c). Fact and fable were submitted to the same test—the test of verisimilitude. The art of the *conteurs* derives from their skill in clothing the fiction in the verisimilar; but in leaving signs of the fictional world visible beneath the trappings of the real world, they call attention to the artistic intent of their work.

3

Sampling the Book: Beginning Metaphors and Their Poetic Function

Likeness, Michael Foucault tells us, played a fundamental role in Renaissance culture.[1] The eye observed in order to compare rather than to draw distinctions, and comprehension took place through the apprehension of known qualities. Béroalde de Verville's prefatory anecdote about those wise and cautious priests who refer to the breviary as their wife offers an apt illustration of Foucault's observation.[2] The metonymic association between priest and breviary or husband and wife gives rise to a metaphor whose humor derives from its illicit implication. Of the four essential figures of likeness or similarity discussed by Foucault as pertinent to Renaissance perception: convenience, emulation, analogy, and sympathy, emulation [*aemulatio*] or metaphor assumes a critical organizational function in the prologues of Renaissance *conteurs*.

Foucault defines emulation as a kind of convenience (resemblance tied to spatial propinquity) but freed from the laws of space.[3] It is likeness without contact, a play of mirror and reflection where distance is unimportant. For man born after the punishment of Babel, the likeness between words and the things they represent is no longer transparent, but hidden. Metaphor, along with the other figures of likeness, signals resemblance in the universe. For Foucault, as for C. S. Peirce, and more recently Hayden White, the metaphor "does not image the thing it seeks to characterize, it gives directions for finding the set of images that are intended to be associated with the thing".[4] Metaphor is a decoding tool. It functions as a symbol, giving neither a verbal description nor a plastic representation of what it represents, "but *tells us* what images to look for in our culturally encoded experience in order to determine how we *should feel* about the thing represented."[5]

The metaphor's status as a symbol, whose meaning is not totally open but oriented towards a precise or conventional meaning, is critical to the role it plays in the prologue. Capable of affecting the way we feel about things—"elle ajoute à nos manières de sentir"—liminary metaphor informs our reception of the text it introduces.[6] A well chosen metaphor can guide a "good" reading of the text to follow more effectively and more economically than the most detailed list of instructions to the reader.[7] Two examples—Rabelais's Silenus box motif (Prologue, *Gargantua*) and Montaigne's portrait motif (Avis au lecteur, *Essais*)—immediately come to mind. One final quality of importance to our study of the use of metaphor in the prologues by Renaissance storytellers is its unexpected, original use, what Paul Ricoeur calls the unexpected application of a label in a new way, a way of teaching new tricks to an old word.[8] Recycling metaphoric expressions—putting old wine in new bottles—was a favorite trick of the Renaissance *préfaciers*, who sought not only to establish familiar ground for the readership but to stake their own claims for innovation. Rabelais is unrivaled in his ability to realize the metaphor's potential to suggest [*pointer*] similarities which remain unexpressed. He draws on the power of the metaphor to develop and expand beyond itself. With the Silenus box metaphor, Rabelais exploits the poetic function of the metaphor to alter the way we look at things.[9] The Silenian metaphor is both rich in itself, because of the play of Platonic and Erasmian intertexts, and in its ability to generate a series of other metaphors based on the exterior/interior opposition: habit/monk, "cappe espagnole"/Spain, bone/marrow.[10] In his enthusiasm to create metaphors, Alcofrybas leaves the strict logic of standard comparison to confuse categories. We are invited to sniff and smell not just the bone but the "beaulx livres de haulte gresse" [these fine and most juicy books] (*Gargantua & Pantagruel:* p. 38). Whether the slip is accidental or intentional, it provides a key to the vast proliferation of metaphors. The inside/outside opposition relates to the reading process. As Gérard Defaux and Raymond La Charité have recently demonstrated, Rabelais's interest in the merits of allegorical interpretation is clearly subordinate to his interest in the reading process and, in particular, in the reception of his text. The Silenian metaphor and the subsequent metaphors it engenders serves to orchestrate a "good reading" of the text.[11] The author's rhetorical goal is a goal shared by almost all *préfaciers*—to persuade the reader to read the book by offering a variety of learned and popular ornaments. In recycling Alcibiades' description of Socrates, enriched by the interplay of the Platonic and Erasmian texts, Rabelais is mindful of the horizon of expectation of his Renaissance readers.[12] His poetic aim is more ambitious in that he sets out to change the way we view the world. This is the expressed goal of the prologue: "Pour tant, interpretez tous mes faictz et mes dictz en la perfectissime partie; ayez en reverence le cerveau caseiforme qui vous paist de ces belles billes vezées, et, à vostre povoir, tenez moy tousjours joyeux" (*Gargantua:* p. 9); [Interpret all my deeds and words, therefore, in the most perfect sense, show deep respect for the cheese-like brain that feeds you on these delicate maggots, and do your best to keep me always merry] (*Gargantua & Pantagruel:* p. 39).

Rabelais's use of the Diogenes metaphor in the prologue to the *Tiers Livre* takes us from the descriptive level, or how to approach the work, to the mythic level. Here we view myth as *fable, mythos,* or narrative configuration in the form of an account.[13] The *préfacier* turns from the descriptive tactic which introduces his praise of Socrates in the *Gargantua* prologue to narration: "Si n'en avez ouy parler, de luy [de Diogenes] vous veulx presentement une histoire narrer" (*Tiers Livre:* p. 394); [If you have never heard of Diogenes, I will tell you a story about him presently] (*Gargantua & Pantagruel:* p. 281). The function of the prologue shifts, as a consequence, from describing or prescribing the way to approach the work to narrating the conditions in which the work was produced. Mentioned in the first sentence of the prologue, the figure of Diogenes serves to put the Renaissance reader on familiar ground, but the entire metaphor (Diogenes/*tonneau* [cask, tub]; *je* [I]/*mon tonneau Diogenic* [my Diogenic cask—the *Tiers Livre*], provides a means by which the author/narrator, writing in his own name, personalizes the literary act of narration.

The fact that both the *Tiers Livre* and *Quart Livre* include extensive narrative passages might suggest to some that he sought greater symmetry between the prologue and the main text. We hasten to add, however, that the lengthy narration of Diogenes' response to the war preparations of the Corinthians leads not so much to the story line of the *Tiers Livre* as to the personal story of the author/narrator. The Diogenic metaphor is a covert means for Rabelais to insinuate himself into the prologue. In his *Livre dou Tresor,* Brunetto Latini describes the covert prologue: "Coverture est quant li parleres met en son prologue mult de paroles entor le fait, et fait semblant que il ne veuille ce que il veult, por aquerir la bienveillance covertement de cels à cui il parole" [Covert narration occurs when the speaker introduces extraneous words concerning the event, and pretends that he doesn't want what he wants, to secretly earn the goodwill of those whom he is addressing].[14] By starting out with the activities of Diogenes, Rabelais satisfies the expectations of his audience for a serious prologue rooted in the textual wealth of Antiquity. Once certain that he has secured the right disposition of his readers, the *préfacier* channels their attention to his own cause: "Je pareillement, quoy que soys hors d'effroy, ne suis toutesfoys hors d'esmoy . . . . Prins ce choys et election, ay pensé ne faire exercice inutile et importun, si je remuois mon tonneau Diogenic" (*Tiers Livre:* pp. 397–98); [In the same way, although I have nothing to fear, I am still not unperturbed . . . . Having made my choice, having made up my mind, I decided that I should perform no useless or tiresome role if I were to tumble my Diogenic tub] (*Gargantua & Pantagruel:* pp. 283–84). Mixing the terms of the metaphor in the same way he had with the bone in the previous prologue, the author/narrator becomes a second Diogenes, even a second Amphion, performing to inspire the work of his fellow citizens. The terms, now confused, allow for a change of focus from Diogenes to his *tonneau*, once empty and soon transformed into an inexhaustible wine cask.[15] While we see the same proliferation of metaphors which had characterized the Silenian metaphor, as the cask becomes in turn the cup of Tantalus, the golden bough, a cornucopia, and Pandora's "bouteille," the original image of Diogenes's barrel becomes unrecognizable in its subsequent transformations. What was originally highlighted—Diogenes's frantic activity against the backdrop of the Corinthians' preparations for invasion—turns into a banquet with eating, drinking, and rejoicing. In the *Gargantua* prologue, each metamorphosis of the initial metaphor leaves the interior/exterior opposition intact. The narrator's taste for amplification takes over in the prologue to the *Tiers Livre*. The internal logic governing the terms of the metaphor gives way to the free play of the prologuist's associative powers.

Unlike Des Périers, who begins the prologue by situating himself in the context of the military rivalry between Francis I and Charles V, Rabelais's narrator approaches self-characterization covertly through the use of two well-known tricks from the Middle Ages: the use of metaphor in its rhetorical function of capturing the attention and goodwill of the audience, and in the use of cultural giants such as Socrates and Diogenes to authorize the text. The Diogenic metaphor leads to a degree of self-revelation by the narrator concerning his stance on the hostilities between the two monarchs ["ceste insigne fable et tragique comedie," *Le Tiers Livre:* p. 398; [this noble interlude and tragic-comedy,] *Gargantua & Pantagruel:* p. 284), and his attitude toward war in general.[16]

It takes yet another metaphor, unrelated to the *tonneau*, to bring the prologue back to its central function of guiding reader reception—the major concern of the earlier prologue to *Gargantua*. The images of the "chameau bactrian" [bactrian camel] and of the "esclave biguarré" [two-colored slave] assume an essentially poetic function as metaphors used not only to embellish but also to illustrate the prologuist's concern for the literary reception of his work. These metaphors pave the way for the introduction of a fundamental quality common to his chosen readers—*Pantagruélisme*, that good-natured approach to the fictional world where nothing shocks: "moienant laquelle jamais en maulvaise partie ne prendront choses quelconques" (*Tiers Livre:* p. 401); [which assures me that they will never take in bad part anything] (*Gargantua & Pantagruel*). The bactrian camel marks the very boundary of a well-disposed reader's tolerance for the unusual.[17] After all, Pantagruel, who embodies tolerance, reproaches Panurge for flouting common usage in his behavior and dress: "Seulement me desplaist la nouveaulté et mespris du commun usaige" (*Tiers Livre:* p. 431); [It is only the novelty and this contempt for common fashion that I dislike] (*Gargantua & Pantagruel:* p. 306). In its poetic function, the bactrian camel flags both the writer's and the reader's awareness of the boundaries of literary invention. Straying too far from established convention will only put off potential buyers.

A sampling of Renaissance prologues indicates to what extent the writers were concerned with the success of their book in the marketplace. Metaphors of the book as merchandise in general, or as a specific commodity—cloth, spice, wine—abound. The clarity and directness of Des Périer's prefatory style shuns elaborate liminary metaphors in favor of direct speech and popular proverbs; yet it perhaps he who most fully develops the analogy between *nouvelles* and perishable commodities. Making a case for local and regional source material of distinctly French origin, as Vigneulles had done before him, Des Périers warns of the damage that can befall source material of foreign or exotic provenance:[18]

> Les nouvelles qui viennent de si loingtain pays avant qu'elles soient rendues sus le lieu, ou elles s'empirent comme le saffran : ou s'encherissent,

comme les draps de soye : ou il s'en pert, la moytié, comme d'espiceries: ou se bouffetent, comme les vins: ou sont falsifies comme les pierreries. Brief, elles sont subgettes à mille inconveniens.

[Before they reach their destination, tales coming from such distant countries deteriorate like saffron or become more expensive, like silk sheets, or diminish by half, like grocery produce, or else swell up like wines or are falsified like precious stones. In short, they are subject to a thousand risks.]

He goes on to add that he prefers to get his source material close at hand. Pleasure is so closely tied to comprehension in the *nouvelle,* a genre dependent on the familiar context and verbal play. What is strange or unfamiliar frightens, as Ptolemé discovered with his bactrian camel. Making a similar argument in favor of producing tales whose distinctly French character stands out, Cholières evokes clothing styles and the French penchant for innovative fashion: "de mesmes qu'entre nous autres Françoys la diversité des habits nous plaist d'autant plus, que celuy que nous avons fait faire tout neuf ne sent rien de l'autre que nous avons laissé." [in the same way that among us Frenchmen, variety in clothes pleases us all the more if what we have had newly fashioned in no way resembles what we have discarded.][19] He blames the diversity of his writing on the French propensity for changing styles. He adds the additional contrast between the man who changes clothes frequently but whose clothes are all cut from the same cloth and in the same style and color ["de mesme estoffe, de mesme façon et de mesme coulleur"] and the courtier who has a different dress for each occasion. Even among the French, taste varies: "on ne doit donc s'esbahir qu'estans François nous avons donné divers habits à nos Après-disnees Françoises" [one ought not to wonder that, being French, we have given different trappings to our French After-dinner Talks] (*Les Après-disnees,* vii r°).

An equally concrete example of the merchandise metaphor can be found in the dedicatory address of Guillaume Bouchet's *Serées* to the merchants of Poitiers. What better way to capture their goodwill than to address them in their own language?

Et vous diray, Messieurs, avec verité, qu'en vous fournissant la marchandise qu'icy je vous presente, je ne me suis en rien esloigné de ceste bonne coustume : vous asseurant, foy de marchand, que je l'ay garnie des meilleures estoffes qui fussent en ma boutique.[20]

> [And I'll tell you, Sirs, in truth, that in supplying you with the merchandise that I show you here, I haven't in the least departed from this good tradition: assuring you, merchant's honor, that I have adorned it with the best fabrics in my shop.]

Appearing before them as a *fournisseur* or supplier, just like his clients, Bouchet gives them more than a small sample [*petit eschantillon*] of his cloth, fully half of the bolt [*la moitié de toute la piece*] for them to try on and check for flaws. Remaking the modesty trope—*excusatio propter infirmitatem*—to fit the commercial context, Bouchet blames his inability to satisfy the tastes of his clients on economic difficulties currently plaguing his store.[21] "Mais s'il se trouve quelques fascheux, n'estans de notre estat, à qui de prime face elle ne plaise, je les prierai d'excuser mon peu de moyen, qui ne me permet avoir en tout mon magazin de meilleur assortiment pour ceste heure" [But if there are some bores not of our ilk, whom it doesn't please at first glance, I beg them to excuse my meager income, which does not permit me at present to have a better selection in my store] (*Serées*, iv). His cry that the stocks are down is also an invitation to come back to sample the second half of the bolt—the next installment of *Serées*—when the supply promises to be richer and more varied. The clever and intimate way in which Bouchet appeals to the merchants of Poitiers gives unity and immediacy to the opening of the *Serées*, qualities we fail to see in the rather dry prologue that follows, not inappropriately named "Discours de l'autheur sur son livre des *Serées*."[22] Instead of viewing literary discourse as a departure from everyday life, Bouchet's opening address to the merchants marks the continuity between the spoken discourse of the market and the written discourse of his *Serées*. Whether his relationship with the merchants is legal or literary, it is based on candor and good will ["candeur et bonne volonté"] (*Les Serées*, v).

Jacques Yver expands the link between written and spoken discourses but by focusing on the enrichment of speech when it is written down and published. To illustrate the superiority of the written word, he opens the first day of the *Printemps* by alluding to the work of a goldsmith on a precious stone—beautiful to begin with, but prettier when set off in gold:

> Comme une pierre précieuse, encore qu'elle porte son prix et valeur avec soi, que sa prodigue mère Nature lui a donné en la produisant et formant,

toutefois se rend plus estimable et riche, quand elle est mise en oeuvre par l'orfèvre industrieux.[23]

[As a precious gem, even though it carries its price and value with it, which its generous Mother Nature bestowed upon it when she brought it forth and formed it, nevertheless increases its value and quality when it is used to advantage by an industrious goldsmith.]

Through his labor, the writer enhances the beauty of his words by setting them off in blessed Memory's temple ["les enchâssant au temple de l'heureuse Mémoire"][24] Memory's temple—the written record—helps preserve the words from oblivion: "ce chien infernal, qui veut engloutir, avec nos corps, la souvenance de notre vie" [this infernal dog which wants to devour, with our bodies, the memory of our life]. The use of artisanal metaphors in the prologues of the *conteurs* can be traced to the supposed "historic" or "lived" provenance of the tale. The storyteller as artisan takes uncrafted, raw material which he or she than crafts but does not invent from pure fancy. The goldsmith metaphor above or Du Fail's image of the carter laboring to bring the words of his peasant neighbors into print (mentioned in Chapter One of this study) illustrate the storyteller's expressed desire to give primacy to verisimilitude over poetic invention.

The idea of finding the appropriate setting or frame for the contents of a work brings to mind Montaigne's artist's metaphor, where the painter selects the center of the wall for the best painting, "élabouré en toute sa suffisance" [labored over with all his skill], and fills the void around it with more primitive and strangely wrought paintings ["crotesques"/"peintures fantasques"].[25] The painting motif found in the middle of the first book of *Essais* echoes the figure of self-portraiture embedded in the notice to the reader at the opening of the book: "Je veus qu'on m'y voie en ma façon simple, naturelle et ordinaire, sans contantion et artifice : car c'est moy que je peins" [I want to be seen here in my simple, natural, ordinary fashion, without straining or artifice; for it is myself that I portray] (*Essais*, "Au lecteur," 9; 3). The metonymic gesture of substituting the friend's artistic endeavor, La Boétie's *Servitude Volontaire*, for his own work conforms completely to the concept of friendship developed in the essay "De l'amitié" (xxviii): "Car cette parfaicte amitié, dequoy je parle, est indivisible; chacun se donne si entier à son amy, qu'il ne luy reste rien à departir ailleurs" [For this perfect friendship I speak of is indivisible: each one gives himself wholly to his friend that he has nothing left to distribute elsewhere] (*Essais*, I, xxviii, 190a; 141). Their wills have become inseparable, one losing itself in the other: "Je dis perdre, à la verité, ne nous reservant rien qui nous fut propre, ny qui fut ou sien, ou mien" [I say lose, in truth, for neither of us reserved anything for himself, nor was anything either his or mine] (187a; 139). Montaigne's self-portraiture and art by La Boétie are one and the same thing, with the slight difference that his friend's work has been labored over with greater attention. The fact that the *Servitude Volontaire* never appeared in the central position and that Montaigne crossed out La Boétie's sonnets in his personal copy of the *Essais*—the famous *exemplaire de Bordeaux*—is not our concern here but perhaps suggests that Montaigne found their styles less compatible than their souls.[26] What is important is the reappearance or renewal of a liminary metaphor to signal another critical passage—the halfway point of the main text. Such a recasting of an opening metaphor functions as an autotext, calling attention to the literarity of the work and obliging the reader to recall and rethink the first half of the work and its generating circumstances—the loss of his friend and the need to continue in another form the commerce he had enjoyed with his friend.[27]

We reserve for last the prologuist who pushes to the limit the power of the metaphor to extend beyond itself. In the above examples, we have seen authors who explore both the rhetorical and poetic functions of the opening metaphor and make full use of its organizational power in the early pages of their work.

In his *Après-disnees*, Cholières creates an entire narrative context around the opening metaphor of his work as godson ["filleul"] and schoolboy ["escolier"]. Much has been written about Cervantes' prefatory claim to be the stepfather rather than the father of *Don Quixote*, a relationship characterized by coolness and distance.[28] Almost twenty years before *Don Quixote*, Cholières describes himself as a sort of substitute godfather for the lively and often capricious schoolboy whose career he is sponsoring. The *préfacier* reminds us that one of the duties of the godfather lies in sponsoring the child in the spiritual and social community—a duty in which the first godfather had been so remiss that the child's name "ne peut estre ramenteu" [cannot be called to memory] (ii r°). The godfather image suggests an affectionate, concerned bond rather than the cold, distant relationship between stepfather and stepson. The new "parrain" [godfather] takes his duties seriously and sets out to find a suitable lodging for his godson/schoolboy: "Je n'estois pas en petite peine, pour sçavoir bien choisir" [I was in no small trouble in knowing how to go about making a good choice.] Our author/narrator shows a talent for child psychology in avoiding the stricter institutional setting for his "escolier" out of fear that he would explode like an unpierced chestnut grilling on the fire: "Mais je cognoissoie son naturel estre tel, que, s'il eust esté resserré dans un college, je le mettoie à l'hazard de crever ou peter *(verba non foetent)* de mesmes que fait une chastaigne mise au feu sans estre fendue" [But I knew his natural disposition to be such that, if he were shut up in a college, I put him at risk of bursting or popping (words don't smell) in the same manner of a chestnut placed on the fire without having been slit] (*Les Après-disnees*, ii v°).

For the reader, there begins to emerge the lively portrait of an active child to whom the benevolent godfather gives a degree of freedom so that the youth's natural disposition will flourish. The expression "je pris deliberation le laisser galocher en martinet" [I resolved to let him find his way as a student-lodger in town] creates the image of a concerned guide who gives a loose rein to his charge. Metaphor, we remember, borrows a lexeme or series of lexemes from a context foreign to the immediate context in order to point to associations, similarities, and thereby to change the way we look at things.[29] Cholières's vivid metaphor, the godfather's struggle to find his schoolboy a lodging, the ill-tempered landlord and his attempt to dislodge the boy from his house, begins to compete with the immediate context of the prologue—the circumstances of publication and the justification for publishing the two works, the *Matinees* and the *Après-disnees*, at the same time. We begin to ask ourselves if we are indeed dealing with a metaphor about the publication of the work or if perhaps we should take the godson/schoolboy story at face value. Ricoeur sees this tension between the literal and figurative meaning as inherent in the poetic function of the metaphor.[30] But if metaphor is in fact an enigma—created by what Ricoeur refers to as a semantic collision—the meaning of the metaphor lies not in the enigma itself, but in its solution.

Instead of going back and forth between the immediate context and the "foreign" context, as Rabelais often does through allusions to the writing process or to the literary or intellectual world of the book, Cholières fully expands his metaphor before returning several pages later to the process of publication. The solution to the enigma comes in the form of another metaphor, echoing the earlier "le laisse galocher en martinet," in which the benevolent godfather lets both boys (his two works) run loose to seek their own fortune: "je me suis advisé (affectionné liseur) que je feroie mieux de leur mettre la bride à l'abandon, afin qu'ils se pourchassent" [I realized (dear reader) that I would do better to give up the bridle so that they could run after each other] (iiii r°). He goes on to say that if they come to harm, they will have him to blame, and if they have good fortune, they'll have only to enjoy it. Should they misbehave, then it will be those who have sewn the seeds of folly who will reap it.

Perhaps the closest parallel to Cholières's metaphor of the two boys is Montaigne's notion of mortgaging his work, appearing not in the 'Au lecteur' but in Book III of the *Essais*. For Cholières, it is better for the author to give the boys/books a loose rein to let them run where they will, whereas Montaigne argues that authority to alter the work ceases at the moment of publication: "J'adjouste, mais je ne corrige pas. Premierement, par ce que celuy qui a hypothecqué au monde son ouvrage, je trouve apparence qu'il n'y aye plus de droict" [I add, but I do not correct. First, because when a man has mortgaged his work to the world, it seems to me that he has no further right to it] (III, ix, 941b; 736). Correcting and revising—as opposed to adding additional material—is like altering merchandise that you have already sold: "Qu'il die, s'il peut, mieux ailleurs, et ne corrompe la besongne qu'il a vendue" [Let him speak better elsewhere, if he can, and not adulterate the work he has sold]. Barry Lydgate suggests that Montaigne uses the "lawyerly verb" *hypothecquer* to convey the importance of protecting the "independent integrity of the work" while at the same time preserving "continuity with its creator."[31]

Cholières extends the liminary metaphor far beyond its traditional organizational role in the prologue. He makes unexpected but no less valid associations between the adult's misgivings about letting go of the child and the author's reluctance to let the work stand on its own merits. What follows the resolution of the metaphor is wholly conventional in terms of justifying the form, substance, and title of his work. But as readers, we will remember his address "aux liseurs" for the valiant efforts of an adoptive godfather to house his rambunctious schoolboy. For the modern reader, experienced in the uncertainties of the publishing world, Cholières's metaphor may still ring a note of truth. He has given us a new strategy for dealing with the dissemination of the printed word.

4
The Functions of the Prologue: A Renaissance View

Having examined specific strategies for organizing the preface—authorization, appropriation, the relationship of truth and fiction, and finally, the use of metaphor—we go on to view the prologue from the global perspective of the various functions performed by the preface. Since Gérard Genette's inventory offers the most complete list of prefatory functions, the list will serve as a point of departure, but efforts will be made to indicate instances when individual prefaces of the Renaissance storytellers chart their own prefatory course.[1]

The principal aim of a preface is to ensure a "good reading" of the work. This is done through a series of functions which Genette groups into the topics of why [les thèmes de pourquoi] and the topics of how [les thèmes de comment] (*Seuils:* p. 183). These themes do not differ greatly from the seven themes or *circumstanciae* set forth by ancient rhetoricians and used to structure many Medieval academic prologues.[2] In order to convince the reader to read the work, the *préfacier* must impress the readers with the value of the subject matter ahead without putting them off by appearing vain or immodest. We recognize here the role of the *captatio benevolentiae* of classical oratory. Theories of rhetoric from both classical and Medieval times stress the role of the *captatio benevolentiae* in the exordium. The writer may stress the *importance* or usefulness of the subject matter, its *novelty*, *unity*, or *truth*.

The genre will, in many instances, determine the functions to be included in the preface. As we discussed earlier, novelty informs both the concept and the structure of the *nouvelle*. The origin of the word can be traced both to the subject of the tale—newsworthy event—and to the act of telling or broadcasting an event. It is anticipated that the teller will renew the material in the process through the addition of a witty, surprise twist at the end—the *pointe* or *trait saillant*.[3] We can foresee, therefore, that the prologues to Renaissance collections of tales will highlight the innovative qualities of the main text.

Beginning well before the start of the sixteenth century, the anonymous author of the Burgundian *Cent Nouvelles Nouvelles*, distances himself from his model, Boccaccio, by pointing to the up-to-date, fashionable quality of his *nouvelles*. In the dedicatory epistle to the Duke of Burgundy which serves as preface, the author writes that his tales have taken place not in Italy, but close at hand, in France, Germany, and Brabant: "l'estoffe, taille et fasson d'icelles est d'assez fresche memoire et de myne beaucoup nouvelle" [their fabric, cut, and styling is of quite recent date and of very new look][4] We remember that Roger Dubuis interprets newness in terms of recent ["fresche memoire"] and in terms of unpublished, novel, newly appearing ["myne nouvelle"].[5] As a guarantee of the freshness of his material, Philippe de Vigneulles stresses the local and regional provenance of his "adventures," many of which he has witnessed himself.[6] So too, Des Périers's preamble to the *Nouvelles Récreations et Joyeux Devis* praises the value of local subject matter which can be delivered fresh to the client before it spoils in transport. The prologuist offers the contemporary example of a local philosopher "le plaisantin" instead of Plato and Xenophon: "Je loueroys beaucoup plus celuy de nostre temps, qui ha esté si plaisant en sa vie que, par une autonomasie, on l'ha appellé le plaisantin" [I would praise all the more our contemporary who was so amusing in his life that, by antonomasia they called him the joker].[7] By the end of the century, vaunting the Frenchness of the tales—their regional specificity—has become an established practice and serves as a guarantee of their fresh, original quality. The Seigneur de Cholières sums up this attitude when he compares the variety and novelty of French literary tastes to the French fascination with changing fashion: "on ne doit donc s'esbahir qu'estans François nous avons donné divers habits à nos Après-disnees Françoyses" [One ought not to wonder that, being French, we have given different trappings to our French After-dinner Talks].[8]

Claims for novelty were widespread although not universal in the prefaces of the Renaissance *conteurs*. The few who underplay innovation, as in the case of Marguerite de Navarre and Rabelais, are those who link their works securely to recognized authors or works of the past. To find a trait common to all the prologues of the Renaissance storytellers in France, we have to look to the claims of moral, historic, and religious significance. Vigneulles bids us to judge importance not by the antiquity of the event but by the storyteller's ability to amplify the event and the circumstances surrounding it.[9] The high sacraments and horrific mysteries promised by Maistre Alcofrybas in the prologue to *Gargantua* are of a documentary nature, covering the economic, political, and religious situation in France.[10] In the *Tiers Livre*, Rabelais narrator offers moral refreshment to take the reader's mind off the impending warfare: "C'est un vray Cornucopie de joyeuseté et raillerie. Si quelque foys vous semble estre expuysé jusques à la lie, non pourtant sera il a sec. Bon espoir y gist au fond" (*Oeuvres complètes* I: p. 402); [It is a true cornucopia of ridicule and fun; and if at times it seems to you to be emptied to the lees, still it will not be dry . . . . good hope lies at the bottom] (*Gargantua & Pantagruel:* p. 286).

One of the benefits of storytelling seems to be its efficacy in boosting morale in adversity. Such diverse authors as Vigneulles, Des Périers, Marguerite de Navarre, Rabelais, Jacques Yver, and Cholières write in response to adverse circusmtances—fever, war, floods, and civil strife. Forced seclusion and leisure can lead to depression, illness, and even death, according to Parlamente and Longarine in the prologue to the *Heptaméron*.[11] Des Périers decides to publish his work before the end of hostilities in order to boost the spirits of his compatriots, "car c'est aux malades qu'il fault medecine" [for it's the sick who need medicine] (*Nouvelles Récréations:* p. 13). Jacques Yver paints a comforting portrait of the people of Poitou picking up the pieces after the third religious war. He describes the Poitevins visiting "les uns les autres, conter et communiquer entre eux leurs pertes et se consoler par la pratique d'un devoir d'amitié en leur commune misère" [one another, recounting and sharing among themselves their losses and consoling each other, by the exercise of friendship's obligations in their common suffering].[12] Literary production is mutually therapeutic for the sender and the receiver.

Claims for the importance of the work and the benefits to be derived from it can undoubtedly lead to hyperbole and facetiousness. In the liminary pages of the *Pantagruel*, Maistre Alcofrybas offers the *Grandes Chroniques* as an antidote for everything from toothache to syphilis. The master of the facetious claims for his work is without a doubt Béroalde de Verville, author of the *Moyen de Parvenir*, a work of from six hundred to nine hundred pages depending on the edition.

Repository of all scientific and philosophical arguments, past, present, and future, "ce joyeux répertoire de perfection, cet antidote contre tout malheur" [this joyous repertory of perfection, this antidote for all misfortune] purports to be the book of books instructing all science in few words.[13] The narrator—we hesitate to say prologuist since Béroalde's strange system of titling does not include a recognizable liminary designation—extends his claims from the known to the occult sciences: "Il embrasse les mystères approuvés de toutes sciences, pour autant qu'il est la juste, solide et naïve interprétation de la pure cabale, de valeur non imaginaire" [It includes the sanctioned mysteries of all sciences, in as much as it is the just, solid, and genuine interpretation of the pure Cabala, whose value is *not* imaginary] (*Le Moyen de Parvenir:* p. 25). The great secret that the narrator passes on to the reader is the book's status as the book to render all other books superfluous: "Ce livre est le centre de tous les livres. Voilà la parole secrette" [This book is the center of all books. That's the secret word] (p. 27). These are lofty claims for a book describes by Gerald Prince as unfit for consumption and unreadable in its unwillingness to give clear directions to the reader and to establish narrative norms.[14]

Genette outlines the argument *a contrario,* a tack that protests that the subject is too trivial to merit the reader's attention.[15] We recognize here, of course, Montaigne's characterization of his self-portrait as a vain and frivolous topic in his notice to the reader: "ce n'est pas raison que tu employes ton loisir en un subject si frivole et si vain" [You would be unreasonable to spend your leisure on so frivolous and vain a subject].[16] Bénigne Poissenot, in *L'Esté* (1583), offers an interesting version of the argument *a contrario,* in which he described his work as a first fruit, the first flight of a fledgling bird out of the nest. Had he wanted to make a greater mark on society, he would have chosen a loftier topic and spent more time revising the work:

> Pour ne te tenir plus longtemps, sçache qu'aucun desir de vaine gloire ne m'a induit à mettre le premier fruict de mon jardin en avant, estant certain que ma renommée ne sortira de longtemps du nid, si je ne l'emplume d'ailes qui puissent mieux fendre l'air que les Icariennes que tu recognois ici.[17]

> [Not to detain you longer, be aware that no desire for vainglory moved me to promote the first fruit of my garden, for I was certain that my renown would not leave the nest for long, if I did not feather it with wings that can cut through the air better than the Icarian wings which you recognize here.]

Rare is the author who repeatedly insists on the recreational value of his work without making at the same time claims for its instructional value. Such is the claim of Poissenot, spurred on by a friend to publish his work: "Mais mon premier but, comme je t'ai prédit, n'estant autre que de me recréer, quelque mien ami m'aiant visité m'incita à faire participer les autres en mes recreations" [But my first goal, as I told you before, being no other than to amuse myself, a friend urged me when he was visiting to engage others in my pleasant pastimes] (*L'Esté:* p. 55).

Of Genette's remaining *thèmes de pourquoi*—topics of unity and truth—the first of these plays only a minor role in the prologues of Renaissance storytellers. On occasion, an author anticipates criticism about the lack of unity, as Cholières does: "Tout ce qui pourroit sembler estrange est, que la suite des matieres n'est liée et enchainée, comme il appartiendroit. De moy, je l'eusse bien souhaité, mais la qualité des personnes et les circonstances du temps ne le permettoient" [All that would possibly seem strange is that the succession of topics is not held together and connected as it ought to be. As for me, I would have wished it so, but the social status of the people and circumstances of the time did not permit it] (*Les Après-disnees*, vi v°). Unlike Montaigne, who blames defects on his own shortcomings—either artistic or mental—Cholières attributes responsibility to external circumstances. Du Fail in turn justifies the modest style of his work by saying that he has left the simple, rustic speech of his villagers unembellished in order to record their daily exchanges more accurately.[18] Presenting a unified work will not become a major concern of the *préfacier* until the seventeenth century.

Truthsaying, on the contrary, is a primary preoccupation of the storyteller, who denies any contradiction between weaving tales and accurately representing events as they occur. The *devisants* in Marguerite de Navarre's *Heptaméron* are careful to distance themselves from Boccaccio in claiming to recount only true stories, a decision handed down to them by the royal family, who had begun the efforts to create a French *Decameron* (*L'Heptaméron:* p. 9). The *nouvelle* as genre requires explicit claims to truthsaying while, at the same time, the pact between narrator and reader demands a complicitous agreement not to challenge the oath of veracity. To strengthen the claim to truth, the Renaissance storyteller often adopts the posture of eye witness. Vigneulles is careful to note that he had learned about ["sceu"], seen ["veu"] for himself, or heard tell ["ouy dire"] of the majority of events in his book from people worthy of trust and belief ["digne de foy et de creance]" *Les Cent Nouvelles Nouvelles:* p. 57). Du Fail inscribes himself in the liminary setting of his work in order to stress his role as eyewitness. Jacques Yver portrays himself as a faithful secretary recording events as they take place: "je me suis remparé de nouvelle hardiesse, sachant que mon but proposé en ce petit récit n'est pas de contrefaire un éloquent orateur; mais bien un fidèle secrétaire qui rapporte les gracieux discours et memorables histoires" [I fortified myself with new courage, knowing that my proposed goal in this modest account is not to imitate an eloquent orator, but rather a faithful secretary who records pleasing conversation and memorable stories] (*Le Printemps:* p. 521). Poissenot equates the truth factor of the established authorized text "d'auteur receu," transmitted in writing, with the oral testimony of "homme digne de foi," a reliable eye witness (*L'Esté:* p. 54).

It is clear that long before Montaigne's "avis au lecteur," good faith was considered a necessary quality for the writer and the book. Several years after the first edition of Montaigne's *Essais*, Bouchet constructs a dedicatory letter to his clients, the merchants of Poitiers, around the concept of good faith as a common criteria for commercial and conversational exchange. First he promises unrestrained and ribald yarns ["discours libres et gaillards"] in the style of their fathers, who went about their work, passing the time by chatting and laughing together ["passans le temps à converser et rire ensemble"].[19] He goes on to propose to his merchants that they enter into a commercial pact, in which he plays the supplier, providing them with cloth. Their pact will be based on good faith and trust, "foy et loyauté, sans laquelle aucun trafic ne peut subsister" [faith and loyalty, without which no trade can go on] (*Les Serées*, iv).

For the Renaissance *conteur*, literary production and dissemination were yet another form of commerce, an institution dependent upon the integrity of the parties involved in the exchange. Even authors whose exaggerated claims were bound to cause skepticism in their audience felt obliged to invoke oaths of veracity. Having blamed all the ills of his time on the introduction of soft balls in the *jeu de paume*, Béroalde de Verville assures us: "et je vous jure sans jurer, que tout est vrai" [and I swear to you without swearing that everything is true] (*Moyen de Parvenir:* p. 2). Another time, he invites us to trust him as the man on the gibbet trusts the hangman not to harm him (p. 29).

Once the writer has convinced the reader of the book's worth and

4: THE FUNCTIONS OF THE PROLOGUE

sincerity, he or she goes on to guide the reader. Such guidance can be given directly, through explicit directions, or by providing the virtual reader with the necessary information to facilitate an informed reading of the text.[20] Here the topics of how [*les thèmes de comment*] come into play: genesis, choice of public, commentary on the title, contract of fiction, order of reading, contextual hints, statement of intention, and, finally, classification of genre.

With the exception of the *Moyen de Parvenir*, the prologues or prefatory statements of the *conteurs* outline the generating circumstances of their works. Seldom seen as a self-generating activity, writing is portrayed as a response to an adverse circumstance: illness (Vigneulles, Cholières, La Motte-Messemé's *Passetemps*); war (Des Périer's *Nouvelles Récréations*, Rabelais's *Tiers Livre*, Yver's *Printemps*); flood (Marguerite de Navarre's *Heptaméron*). Much has been said of Montaigne's writing as a compensatory exercise after the death of La Boétie.

In the background of these works is of course the *Decameron*, Boccaccio's response to the plague in Florence, yet one wonders with Edward Said if storytelling does not have at its origin the fear of the void—the need to provide alternate compensatory forms of existence.[21] In her dedicatory letter to her cousin, "Madame Jeanne Flore" dates the generation of stories in her *Contes Amoureux* from more pleasant circumstances, the grape harvest.[22] All of these circumstances, whether adverse or pleasurable, interrupt the normal rhythm of life, and narration is seen as a means of filling the time productively until normal activity resumes.

The *Moyen de Parvenir* is unique in its refusal to either explain its beginning or to effect its own closure. The narrator gives no justification for the strange gathering of luminaries from over the centuries other than the love of dialogue and laughter. Gerald Prince tells us that the text refuses to claim for itself a single origin or paternity.[23] Perhaps its status as the Book of Books demands that it resist historic classification in a single literary period.

If the storytellers are generally firm in the need to outline the generating circumstances of their work, their response to the second function outlined by Genette—the designation of a chosen public—is much more varied. Three concurrent phenomena made the authors increasingly sensitive to the reception of their works: the expanding commerce in books, the rise in unauthorized editions of books, and the censorship of the printed word by the Church. The writer's uneasiness concerning the reception of his work marks particularly the liminary pages of the book.

We need only contrast the dedicatory letter of the Burgundian *Cent Nouvelles Nouvelles*, confident and secure as it addresses the patron whose literary tastes were most certainly known to the author, with the prefaces of later Renaissance works. The anonymous author's humble prayer that his gift be received with pleasure ["agreablement . . . reçu"] contains no hint of anxiety about the eventual reception of the work (*Cent Nouvelles Nouvelles:* p. 19). We see the same simplicity and straightforward quality in the incomplete prologue of Vigneulle's work of same name (1515) and in Nicolas de Troyes's second volume of the *Grand Parangon* (1535–37).[24] Neither author fleshes out the character of the readers addressed, but Philippe de Vigneulles adds that he hopes his tales will inspire "tous ceulx et celles qui les liront ou orront" [all those men and women who will read and hear them] to compose tales in their turn, so it is clear that he is addressing a mixed readership (*Cent Nouvelles Nouvelles*, p. 57).

In the third and fourth decades of the sixteenth century, Des Périers and Rabelais begin to paint a philosophical portrait of their readership—an image describing not men and women of a given social class or profession but a philosophical profile of their favored readers. Their technique fits in nicely with the topics of how, for they describe the disposition required for approaching the work in the right state of mind. Des Périers and Rabelais are very close in prescribing a positive outlook unaffected by events beyond human control.[25] Des Périers is quick to recognize that his female audience must keep up appearances and so suggests that they pretend not to listen: "Mais je suis content que devant les gens elles facent semblant de couldre ou de filler: pourveu qu'en destournant les yeulx, elles ouvrent les oreilles" [But I'm satisfied if in front of others they pretend to sew or spin, provided that in averting their eyes, they open their ears] (*Nouvelles Récréations:* p. 17). The well-disposed reader will approach the work with honesty and loyalty, and in return will be rewarded with joy and laughter:

> Tout Beuveur de bien, tout Goutteux de bien, alterez, venens à ce mien tonneau, s'ilz ne voulent, ne beuvent; s'ilz voulent et le vin plaist au guoust de la seigneurie de leurs signeuries, beuvent franchement, librement, hardiment sans rien payer, et ne l'espargnent." (*Tiers Livre:* p. 402)

[Every honest boozer, every decent gouty gentleman, everyone who is dry, may come to this barrel of mine, but need drink only if he wishes. If they wish, and the wine is to the taste of their worshipful worships, let them drink frankly, freely, boldly, and without stint or payment.] (*Gargantua & Pantagruel:* p. 286)

Whereas Des Périers concentrates on developing the positive disposition of his readers, Rabelais excoriates the would-be critics and censors. In the *Pantagruel*, Alcofrybas reserves his venom for the skeptics among his readers. It is in the *Tiers Livre* that Rabelais paints the most vivid picture of those he excludes from his readership—the "grabeleurs de corrections" ['high-hatted pettifoggers']—the censors who read to find fault rather than enjoyment: "Venez vous icy culletans articuler mon vin et compisser mon tonneau?" (*Tiers Livre:* p. 403); [So you have come here, wagging your tails, to sniff at my wine, and piss in my barrel, have you?] (*Gargantua & Pantagruel:* p. 287). Wariness toward an expanding readership whose make up is uncertain gives way to a cry of indignation against the clerics who take unnatural pleasure in misreading texts and distorting authorial intention: "Gzz. gzzz.gzzzz. Davant davant! Iront ilz? Jamais ne puissiez vous fianter que à sanglades d'estrivières, jamais pisser que à l'estrapade, jamais eschauffer que à coups de baston!" (*Tiers Livre:* p. 403); [Gzz, gzz, gzzz. Off with you! Off with you! Are they not gone yet? May you never manage a shit without being lashed with stirrup leathers, may you never squeeze out a piddle without being strappadoed, and may your body never be warmed except by a great hiding!] (*Gargantua & Pantagruel:* p. 287). At the end of the century, Béroalde de Verville excludes the same hypocritical readers: "gardez-vous de ces entrelardeurs de Theologie alegorique . . . et de tous ceux qui aiguisent leurs remonstrances sur la meule d'hypocrisie" [beware of these mixers of allegorical theology , . . . and of those who hone their reprimands on the grindstone of hypocrisy] (*Le Moyen de Parvenir:* p. 27). He reserves his secrets for the good people who enjoy good reading without taking offense.

More moderate in his approach to potential critics but increasingly cynical about the possibility of satisfying the growing expectations of the reading public, Jacques Yver creates a culinary metaphor to explain the writer's dilemma. Just as the culinary tastes of the public have grown more refined, so too has its literary taste, and Yver despairs of ever finding the right ingredients to enrich his sauce, "sachant les esprits de notre siècle être si dégoûtés d'un fade dédain, qu'il n'y a sauce si exquise qui les puisse mettre en bon appétit" [knowing the intellects of our century to be so squeamish from a weak distaste that there is no sauce so choice that could restore their appetite] (*Printemps:* p. 521). He speaks of letting these difficult readers know that the fault that they find with the meat is actually in themselves ["que le blâme qu'ils donnet à la viande est en eux-mêmes"]. Faultfinding takes on a specular quality, in which the flaws present in the object consumed reflect character flaws in the consumer. Yver takes heart in the merit of his own enterprise and pays no more heed to the fickle tastes of jaded readers.

Although the text is always in the process of inviting a response, prologuists differ as to their degree of involvement with the specific character of their reading public.[26] While some prologuists are silent on the subject of their chosen readers—Marguerite de Navarre (*L'Heptaméron*) and Noël du Fail (*Propos rustiques*), others seem obsessed by the subject of reader reception. In dedicating his book to those he has served as *juge-consul*—the merchants of Poitiers, Bouchet limits the primary audience for whom he writes and, as a consequence, can more precisely dictate the rules of the game. He writes for a social group whose faith and loyalty has been less affected than most by the religious wars. The "foy de marchand" or merchant's oath of trust and loyalty remains operative in the fictional contract between narrator and reader. Thoroughly familiar with the good will and candor of his clients ["cognaissant vostre candeur et bonne volonté," *Les Serées:* p. ix), he writes with the certainty that his goods will please.

As the preface ["Discours de l'autheur sur son livre de Serées"] opens, frequent references to possible criticism reveal a certain wariness toward the reader. Genette names such mention of future criticism lightning rods ["paratonnerres"]—a protective device for warding off or preempting possible criticism.[27] Bouchet protests, "Et si vous m'alleguez qu'en ces banquets ny en leurs Serees, il n'y a pas gueres de temps pour dire et apprendre beaucoup de choses, je vous respondray qu'il y en a bien assez, estant employé comme font les gens sçavans, qui n'en perdent une seule minute" [And if you argue that in these banquets and in their Evening Gatherings, there is hardly any time to say and learn much, I'll answer you that there is quite enough, put to use in the manner of learned people who never waste a single moment] (*Les Serées:* p. ix). Each potential criticism is met with a defense from the wise and learned people ["sages et sçavans"].

4: THE FUNCTIONS OF THE PROLOGUE

To those who would accuse him of having borrowed excessively from other authors, he would offer Seneca's reply all good things are common property (p. xii). He borrows like someone whose friend has entrusted him with money before leaving on a trip. He uses the money until the friend returns. Bouchet blames the presence of facetious and merry topics on his lack of knowledge and incompetence at writing serious thoughts. He is only imitating "les amoureux de Penelopes, lesquels ne pouvans jouyr de la maistresse, se mirent apres les chambrières" [the lovers of Penelope, who, unable to seduce the mistress, go after the maid servants] (*les Serées*: p. xiii). His readers are as guilty as he is for mixing learned and serious topics with ribald pastimes ["propos doctes et serieux, avec les plaisirs gaillards"], for in reading the work, they have made themselves accomplices in the literary pact.[28] For Bouchet, the contract between writer and reader is not unlike that between buyer and seller, in which both parties are implicated in the exchange.

The notion of contract brings us to another of Genette's functions—the fictional contract.[29] Unfortunately, Genette's treatment of the fictional contract deals principally with works appearing after the Renaissance and so concentrates on the oath of fictionality rather than the oath of veracity and the sometimes subtle, sometimes overt unveiling of the fictional underpinnings of the work. William Nelson has perhaps best characterized the contract between Renaissance storyteller and reader: "But the proper relationship between author and his audience required a mutual understanding that the story was neither history told 'for true' nor a childish confusion of make-believe with real, but a transparent device calculated to appeal to a less-than-serious aspect of human nature."[30] Rabelais invites us to enter into his fictional contract when he claims in *Pantagruel* that the *Grandes et inestimables Chroniques de l'énorme géant Gargantua* have sold more copies in two months than the Bible in nine years.[31] His promise to reveal high sacraments and horrific mysteries about the religious, political, and economic life is but a facetious way of justifying the recreative aspects of the work to follow (*Gargantua*: p. 8). Understating the aesthetic and recreative value of narrative in favor of the moral or intellectual instruction to be derived from it played an essential part of the contract between writer and reader.[32] The Silenus box and the "substantial marrow" ["sustantificque mouelle"] function as lures in the liminary pages of *Gargantua*. The narrator becomes the reader's accomplice in providing a learned pretext for a shockingly pleasurable experience. Gargantua's birth through his mother's left ear is just the narrator's reminder not to take the liminary promise too seriously. The fact that Béroalde de Verville's inflated praise of his work—"ce docte monument, ce précieux memorial, ce joyeux repertoire de perfection" [this learned monument, this precious memorial, this joyous repertory of perfection]—appears a few pages after the detailed description of Marciole's anatomy, as she stoops stark naked to pick up cherries in front of a group of appreciative gentlemen, can only be taken as an invitation to the reader to participate in the fictional contract (*Moyen de Parvenir:* pp. 14–23).

Of the *conteurs* whose collections of tales and "propos" we are considering, only Des Périers openly points to the fictional basis of his work, a practice so common in later centuries. "Et puis j'ay voulu faindre quelques noms tout expres pour vous monstrer qu'il ne faut point plorer de tout cecy que je vous compte: car peult estre qu'il n'est pas vray" [And so I wanted to make up several names precisely to show you that you shouldn't cry over all that I tell you, for perhaps it's not true] (*Nouvelles Récréations:* pp. 15–16). Narrative, and in particular the *nouvelle*, was so steeped in the convention of the eyewitness account that authors of the most inventive tales felt obliged to insist on the truth of their account. The contract of fictionality had to be revealed in an indirect fashion. Rabelais's facetious use of statistics—the number of Utopians transported to colonize Dipsodie (9876543210) or the number of cows required to provide milk for the infant Gargantua ("dix et sept mille neuf cens treze vaches" [17,913 cows]) allows him to play at verisimilitude while reassuring the reader that the fictional contract is still operative.

Of the remaining functions outlined by Genette, some are more pertinent than others to Renaissance prologues, but all are present. Genette indicates that the prefactory function of defining the genre is most apt to be used in works whose genre is not clear or in works written in periods of transition, where old generic labels are no longer applicable.[33] With the notable exception of Montaigne's notice to the reader, which comments neither on the genre of his work, except to class it as self-portraiture, nor on its unusual title, Genette's statement holds true in the Renaissance, particularly in works in which dialogue begins to assume the role played by narration.[34] The function of defining the genre of a work is most often associated with another function: commentary on the title. Genette does not mention this connection, but the link is pertinent to all discussions of the Renaissance prologue. We see the *préfaciers* struggling not only to justify the genre in which they are writing but to explain their choice of title. New genres demand new titles. Works which clearly fit into the classification of short or extended narrative: the *Cent Nouvelles Nouvelles* of Vigneulles, Rabelais's works, the *Nouvelles Récréations,* or the *Heptaméron,* need little commentary on the title. The reader has had ample experience with collections of tales. As dialogue begins to vie for space with narrative episodes in a period characterized by the popularity of neoplatonism and dialectic, more titles are invented to stress the dialogic tone of the works, and the prologuist devotes more time to the explanation of both the genre and the title of the work.

Noël du Fail devotes an entire preface to explaining his use of *rustique* in the title. Rusticity means many things: the bestial existence characteristic of prehistoric man; the poor peasant class who could not afford to pay poets to sing its praises; the useful, hardworking crowd whom Cicero praised as good people ("Au lecteur," *Propos rustiques:* pp. 601–5). Du Fail's long preamble prepares his reader for the simple style in which the work is written and for the unusual protagonists in his collection of conversations and anecdotes. The generic expectations of his readers necessitate some sort of preparation by Du Fail. We are not to expect a gathering of genteel courtiers or bourgeois merchants:

> Contente toy donc (amy lecteur) de ce peu que je te offre, chose (soubz ton jugement soit) indisposee et de mauvaise grace, toutesfois en observant lhonneur et droict de escrire choses basses et humbles, ne requierent style eslevé, ne grand façon de dire, tel mercier tel panier. (*Propos rustiques:* p. 605)

> [Be satisfied (reader friend) with this pittance that I offer you, an object which you esteem to be ill wrought and unattractive. Bearing in mind, however, that the honor and privilege of writing about low and humble things do not require elevated style nor lofty expression, let the basket suit the haberdasher.]

Reverting to the conventional opposition between high and low style, he justifies both his title and his innovative treatment of a genre previously devoted to the depiction of courtly and urban events.

The authors of the so-called "recueils bigarrés" [mixed collections of conversations and anecdotes] resort to lengthy prefatory statements explaining both their choice of title (*Après-disnees, Serées, Passetemps*) and the genre to which the work belongs. Cholières assures us that his *Après-disnees* belong to the tradition of philosophical exercises "introduits par l'Antiquité" (*Après-disnees*, v r°). He cites the example of Alphonse, King of Aragon, who summoned learned men to his court to converse after dinner. To justify the light nature of his work, he gives the example of the Emperor Hadrian, who preferred the company of actors and poets after dinner so that he might be cheered and refreshed ["regaillardis et recreez"] by the performers' singing and merriment.

Bouchet reminds the reader of the double origin of his work—French narrative and classical dialogue—by insisting upon the association between French custom and classical literary practice. His explicit mention of the link removes his work from the fringes of both genres and carves a place for the work at the confluence of the two traditions:

> Parquoy je ne me sçaurois saouler de loüer l'honneste coustume et façon de vivre, de laquelle lon use en plusieurs villes de nostre France, où les parens, amis et voisins s'accordent à porter chacun son petit ordinaire en la maison, tantost de l'un, tantost de l'autre. . . . Ce qui a esté cause que les Grecs ont appellé ces convis, *Symposia philetica*, et les Latins *amica convivia*, c'est à dire, banquets d'amis." (*Serées:* p. vi)

> [For this reason, I never tire of praising the honest custom and practice which goes on in many towns in our France, where relatives, friends, and neighbors agree each to carry his food sometimes to one person's house sometimes to another's. . . . Which gave cause to the Greeks to call these suppers *Symposia philetica*, and the Romans, *amica convivia*, that is to say, friends' feasts.]

Having clarified the generic classification in a serious tone, Bouchet assumes a lighter tone to explain his title. In an echo of Rabelais's prologue to *Gargantua*, he explains that the title *(Serées)* is enough to suggest why his book smells more of wine than of oil. At the very worst, the title might be used as reason to classify the work among the "old wives" tales told to cackling women and maids as they spin, "pour recreer l'esprit, qui apres le manger et le boire est plus subtil et gaillard" [to refresh the mind, which after eat and drink, is more subtle and alert] (*Serées:* p. xxvi).

In a more cynical tone, Bouchet goes on to say that all prefatory defenses are useless, for even Heraclides could not defend the title of his work against defamation and mockery.[35] At least, he argues, his straightforward title gives a hint of the context of the work, unlike

4: THE FUNCTIONS OF THE PROLOGUE

other haughty titles ["superbes titres"]. Bouchet's long discussion of the origins and the placement of his work in French culture and in the long literary tradition which began with the ancients and continues through the sixteenth century indicates the extent of his concern for the literary reception of his work. The king of the "paratonnerre" [lightning rod], he tries to foresee and forestall all manner of criticism in his preface, yet he sees and discusses openly the futility of his efforts. This last revelation leads Bouchet to invent a more efficient means of dealing with critics who would defame his work or publish unauthorized editions. He has printed it with ink composed of a mixture of absinthe and wild cucumber juice. The practical use of his work for wrapping food or personal hygiene will result in physical harm to the user: "Voire mesmes ceux qui le feront servir à un usage encores plus vil, au lieu que les anciens, avant l'invention du papier, usoient d'esponges, en sentiront une grande dyssenterie et excoriation ès parties plus cachees et possible la mort" [Indeed even those who'll put it to a still baser use, in the place where the ancients used sponges before the invention of paper, they'll experience a serious case of dysentery and shredding of skin in their most private parts and maybe even death] (*Serées:* p. xxvi). Let the buyer beware! This *préfacier* has developed the ultimate protection for his work.

Before addressing the final and most important function of he preface—the declaration of intention—let us pass briefly over two functions that play only a minor role in the prologues of Renaissance *conteurs*. Advice on the order in which the work should be read is rare in the prefatory pages, but Béroalde de Verville, whose chapter headings reveal his playful attitude toward textual order, tells us that his work has no particular order. To illustrate the fact, he recounts the story of the "bon homme Guyon" who had been in turn a royal page, a Franciscan, a Huguenot, a learned man, a minister, and who, at the age of one hundred, began to live with the austerity of a Capuchin monk. People mixed all kinds of food and drink together in his bowl. When asked why he didn't eat each course separately, he replies that since the food gets mixed up in his belly, there is no danger in sending it down to the belly already mixed:

> Le personnage qui vous produit en tout honneur ces sainctcs memoires de perfection, a pensé que le texte ne valloit mieux que le commentaire , parquoy il les a fait aller ensemble . . . . Donques soit que vous le lisiez ou non, ou que vous commenciez icy ou là, n'importe, ce livre est par tout plein de fidelles instructions." (*Le Moyen de Parvenir:* p. 18)

[The person who, with all due respect, brings out these holy memoirs of perfection for you, thought that the text was no better than the commentary, and so he has put them together . . . . So whether you read it or not, or whether you begin here or there, no matter, this book is filled with faithful instructions throughout.]

As if to prove the arbitrary order of his work, his headings have no apparent sequence. "Pause dernière" [final pause] and "conclusion" come early on in the book.[36] "Dessein" [purpose], which might appear properly in the very first pages, introduces a narrative rather than an expository segment. Gerald Prince has ably demonstrated that order, as seen in the origin and the completion of the message, is not the subject of the *Moyen de Parvenir*. Freed as it is from the closed circuit of communication and transgressing the boundaries of logic, language in the *Moyen de Parvenir* becomes the locus of the possible at every instant ["le lieu du possible à chaque instant"].[37] Béroalde frees the preface, along with the work, of its explanatory function. In the *Moyen de Parvenir*, the functions of the preface are thwarted by the opacity of the written word. Although individual dialogues and anecdotes are comprehensible, it is the disordered mass of words which impedes the process of global comprehension.

One way in which the narrator may choose to orient his reader is to set the present work in the context of his or her other works. A device practiced especially in the late nineteenth century when new works were sometimes serialized in periodicals, the practice is rare but not unknown among Renaissance storytellers. Montaigne speaks of his writing effort in general rather than tying the "avis au lecteur" to a specific edition of the *Essais*. Rabelais runs through a list of his works—some real, some invented—to recall their content and to chide them for judging books on the basis of their titles:

"Par autant que vous, mes bons disciples, et quelques aultres foulz de sejour, lisans les joyeulx titltres d'aulcuns livres de nostre invention, comme *Gargantua, Pantagruel, Fessepinte, La Dignité des Braguetttes, Des Poys au lard cum commento*, etc., jugez trop facilement ne estre au dedans traicté que mocqueries, folateries et menteries joyeuses, veu que l'ensigne exteriore (c'est le tiltre) sans plus avant enquerir est communement receu à derision et gaudisserie." (*Gargantua:* p. 6)

[It is that you, my good disciples and other leisured fools, in reading the pleasant titles of certain books of our invention, such as *Gargantua, Pantagruel, Toss-Pint, On the Dignity of Codpieces, Of Peas and Bacon, cum commento*, &c, may not too easily conclude that they treat of nothing but mockery, fooling, and pleasant fictions; seeing that their outward signs—their titles, that is—are commonly greeted , without further investigation, with smiles of derision.] (*Gargantua & Pantagruel:* p. 37)

Prior to revealing his intention in writing the *Après-disnees*, Cholières tells us that we must become familiar with something before liking it, lest we be surprised; it is best to know the origins of the object that falls into our hands: "Il faut (dit on) cognoistre avant qu'aimer, de peine d'estre surpris, il est bien seant que sçachez, d'où c'est, que vous vient ce qui tombe en vos mains" (*Après-disnees*, iiii v°). Cholières clearly perceives the importance of the liminary pages of the text in engaging the public and convincing the reader to read on into the main text. Antoine Compagnon has described how, since the sixteenth century, the reader judges the receivability of the text on the "périgraphie" [perigraphy] of the main text: notes, tables, preface, foreword, appendix.[38] He compares the *périgraphie* to shop windows, photo proofs, or free samples.

We cannot say, however, that the liminary space serves as a locus of advertisement for past or future works. Rabelais and Cholières are exceptional among the *conteurs* in this regard. A far more critical use of liminary space can be found in the declaration of intention. Among the storytellers whose works we are discussing, I am not sure that it deserves the status of the most important function accorded it by Genette; yet it plays an essential prefatory role.[39] All of the prologuists in question give at least lip service to Horace's rule that the work must both please and instruct. Perhaps because of the genre, they are most convincing in their promise to give pleasure, and their vow to instruct appears at times forced or ironic. An exception could be made for Hélisenne de Crenne, whose dedicatory letter addressed "à toutes honnestes dames" [to all good ladies] recalls Boccaccio in speaking as an unhappy lover who writes so that other lovers may be spared pain and suffering: "O trescheres dames, quand je considere qu'en voyant comme j'ay esté surprise, vous pourrez eviter les dangereux lacqs d'amour, en y resistant du commencement, sans continuer en amoureuses pensées" [O very dear ladies, when I consider that, seeing how I was surprised, you will be able to avoid the dangerous snares of love by resisting it from the beginning without persisting in amorous thoughts].[40] Another dedicatory letter addressed not to a group of women but to a single woman by her cousin, Jeanne Flore, mentions nothing about instruction but stresses the pleasure giving nature of her gift, the transcription of the *Contes Amoureux*. She notes that she would be doing something very agreeable and pleasant ["chose tres agreable et plaisante"] by publishing such joyous tales ["telz joyeulx comptes"] (*Contes Amoureux:* p. 97).

Marguerite de Navarre opens her prologue with a declaration of intention, but the narrator, in a rare moment of direct address to the reader, mentions neither pleasure nor instruction: "Ma fin n'est de vous declarer la scituation ne la vertu desdits baings, mais seullement de racompter ce qui sert à la matiere que je veulx escripre" [My object is not to speak to you about the location or the merits of these baths, but only to recount what relates to the subject that I want to write about] (*L'Heptaméron:* p. 1). She vows only to recount faithfully the essential elements of the narrative. Her intention is perhaps in line with the intention of the originators of the project, the royal family, who pledged to tell only true stories. As for the intention of the secondary narrators, her storytellers, they are most assuredly intent upon enjoying themselves in the process of whiling away the time required for the flood to subside. Hircan, after all, invites his wife Parlamente to propose a pastime "où chascun prendra plaisir" [in which each one will take pleasure] (p. 9).

Rabelais's shift from writing to provide pleasure and entertainment for his readers in *Pantagruel* to revealing the secrets and mysteries of the religious, political, and economic life in France has perhaps less to do with the actual content of his work than with the literary tastes and expectations of his readers. By promising instruction and revelation in *Gargantua*, he appeals to a more learned clientèle. In the *Tiers Livre*, his avowed intention to serve his compatriots by writing sets him in the august company of the classical philosophers, yet his amplification of the subject matter contained within the work makes it clear that we have no hidden mysteries but entertainment to cheer up his beleaguered countrymen. He promises "un guallant tiercin et consecutivement un joyeulx quart de sentences Pantagruelicques" (*Tiers Livre:* p. 400); [a gallant third draught—and later a jovial fourth—of Pantagrueline Sentences' (*Gargantua & Pantagruel:* p. 285). The images of the cask ["tonneau"] and the cornucopia of ridicule and fun ["cornucopie de joyeuseté et raillerie"] suggest refreshment, recreation, and inspiration more than instruction and self-improvement (p. 402; p. 286). Rabelais's prefatory statements increasingly favor the giving of pleasure over the instructional element. The enhanced role given to narration in his prologues reveals an awareness that the best way to give the reader a sampling of his work is to begin telling stories in the liminary space of the prologue. In the prologue to the *Quart Livre*, his talk of health and moderation is a means of preparing the reader both physically and mentally to better enjoy his work: "Or, en bonne santé toussez un bon coup, beuvez en trois, secouez dehait vos aureilles, et vous oyrez dire merveilles du noble et bon Pantagruel" (*Oeuvres complètes* II, p. 29); [So then, since you are in good health, give a good cough for me, toss off three bumpers, give your ears a good shake, and you shall hear marvels of the noble and excellent Pantagruel] (*Gargantua & Pantagruel:* p. 449).[41] Narration and instruction go hand in hand, but without the right disposition, they fall on deaf ears.

Des Périers is unequivocal in denying higher, more serious instructive aims for his work: "Mais sçavez vous quelz je les vous baille? Je vous prometz que je n'y songe ny mal ny malice : il n'y ha point de sens allegoricque, mistique, fantastique" [But do you know which ones I'm offering you? I promise you that I am concocting neither evil nor malice; there is no allegorical, mystical, or supernatural meaning] (*Nouvelles Récréations:* p. 15). Yet bringing joy to people is in itself a sort of instruction: "Le plus grand enseignement pour la vie, c'est *Bene vivere et laetari*" [The greatest instruction for living is to live well and rejoice] (p. 14). As we have commented earlier, Plainsantin's humorous approach to death, recounted at the end of the preamble, serves to illustrate this motto.

Instruction is only important for Cholières in defending lighter, pleasing discussions against the rigors of more serious philosophical debate. Yet the efficacy of instruction is intimately linked to the pleasurable way it is delivered. The learning process must be pleasurable in itself: "Il me fascheroit fort de pleiger aucun, si est ce que je me promets, que bien peu s'esbattroit apres mes Après-disnees, qu'incontinant ils n'en retirent du plaisir de la doctrine et de l'utilité" [It would vex me greatly to promise someone, just as I promise myself, that he would not dally long at my After-dinner Chats before soon taking delight in its instruction and usefulness] (*Après-disnees*, vi v°). Again and again he urges his readers to enjoy his work: "Tenez, je vais vous représenter le dessein de ces discours, à celle fin qu'avec plus grande gayeté de coeur vous vous esgayez en ces gayes Apres-disnees" [Wait, I'm going to show you the purpose of these talks, so that, with greater lightness of heart, you cheer up with these lively After-dinner Chats]. It becomes apparent that his design is to give pleasure, and that to this end, he evokes, as Bonaventure Des Périers had done, the *laetari et bene vivere* motto: "et vous souvenez que veut la pratique de cet Axiome, *laetari et bene vivere*" [and remember the meaning of the practice of this axiom, *laetari et bene vivere*] (vii r°).

At first glance, Bouchet's opening "Discours" to the *Serées* appears to be entirely devoted to intellectual matters: "Mais laissant à part la refection du corps, comme la chose moins considerable en ces banquets, j'estime plus la refection et contentement de l'esprit" [But leaving aside the sustenance of the body, as of smallest consequence in these banquets, I give greater value to the sustenance and satisfaction of the mind] (*Serées:* p. viii). But as the discourse continues, refection and enjoyment are increasingly connected to laughter. A philosopher retains his status as a wise and learned man even when he is playing and bringing joy to others (p. x–xi). Like Cholières, Bouchet believes that pleasure facilitates learning:

> Et que sçay-je si on pourra point dire de ces Serées, comme quelqu'un a laissé par escrit de ses oeuvres? Et pourrez, vous sçavans, quelque plaisir y prendre: Vous, non sçavans, pourrez en riant y apprendre. (*Serées:* p. xiii)

> [And how do I know if one couldn't say about these Evening Chats, as someone has written about his own works? 'And may you, learned people, take pleasure in them. You, unlearned people, may you learn from them while laughing.']

Bouchet's prefatory discourse is, in fact, a discourse not on how to run a symposium but on the benefits of laughter in life. The critics of his books will be those who disapprove of his primary intention in writing—to make people laugh. With Aristotle and Rabelais, he views laughter as the "propre de l'homme" [the quality distinctly belonging to man] (p. xvii). His critics, by extension, are "missantropes." For these enemies of mankind, he devises, we recall, an equally inhumane antidote—poison ink. What had appeared to be a serious defense of the symposium is transformed into a praise of laughter and its positive effects on the mind and body.

Bouchet's solution to the problem of hostile critics reveals an underlying skepticism about the power of the preface or other paratextual forms to ward off criticism and to guarantee a "good" reading of the text. No declaration of good intention can ensure a single reading of the text nor silence criticism, as Cholières reminds us: "En un mot, l'amour et affection que je porte à mon pays, ne garentira de tout le reproche qu'on me pourroit donner" [In a word, the love and affection that I bear for my country will not in the least shield me from criticism that might be aimed at me] (*Après-disnees*, viii r°).

Writing within a century of the invention of printing, the Renaissance *conteurs* were already keenly aware of the breakdown in communication which results in the process of disseminating the printed word. The prefatory apparatus is an attempt to impede this breakdown. Jacques Derrida has described the preface as the utterance of the father: "As the preface to a book, it is the word of a father assisting and admiring his work, answering for his son, losing his breath in sustaining, retaining, idealizing, reinternalizing, and mastering his seed."[42]

But as the word goes out, and the book is published and circulated, people will bring their own background and expectations to the work. The *préfacier* cannot possibly foresee the various interpretations which will be applied to the book. "Croiez vous en vostre foy qu'oncques Homere, escrivent l'*Iliade* et *Odyssée*, pensast es allegories lesquelles de luy ont calfreté Plutarche, Heraclides Ponticq, Eustatie, Phornute, et ce que d'iceulx Politian a desrobé?" (*Gargantua:* p. 8); [But do you faithfully believe that Homer, in writing his *Iliad* and *Odyssey*, ever had in mind the allegories squeezed out of him by Plutarch, Heraclides, Eustathius, and Phornutus, and which Politian afterwards stole from them in his turn?' (*Gargantua & Pantagruel:* p. 38)]. In spite of his genius for writing prologues, Rabelais suffered greatly from those who would accuse him of sinister intentions.

With the development of the preface in the sixteenth century comes an increased skepticism as to whether it was a worthwhile activity. As prefaces expand and assume more varied forms, they become more self-reflective on the prefatory process in progress. Cervantes' prologue to *Don Quixote de la Mancha* is perhaps the most famous example of such self-reflection.[43] We cannot say with Genette that the declaration of intention is more important than other prefatory functions in the Renaissance. In fact, in perhaps the most structured and direct prologue of the Renaissance *conteurs*, the preface to Poissenot's *Esté* skirts the issue of intention. He includes many of the prefatory functions mentioned above: he follows tradition as well as an established genre—the *facétie;* he models his work after that of a known "autheur," Jacques Yver, excuses his lack of polish, and still has time to comment on the genesis of the work and the title. In its concise structure, Poissenot's preface—entitled *préface* and not *prologue* or *avis au lecteur*—announces the tidy prefaces which will become standard in later centuries. There are no digressions into narrative or long discussions so commonplace in other Renaissance prologues.

Yet there is a distinct vagueness in his discussion of motivation for writing. He begins by stating that he writes to lighten his mind weighed down by a heavy burden, "pour soulager mon esprit aggravé de pesant faix qui le chargeoit" (*L'Esté:* p. 52). He repeats the statement of intention: "car, mon intention n'estant au commencement autre que me tirer des cogitations qui me rendoient sombre et tenebreux" [for my intention at the outset was only to pull myself out of those considerations which made me somber and grave] (pp. 52-53). He gives us no further explanation or guidelines for understanding the content of his work. In addition, he undermines any loftier intention by telling us that he had only reread the work once before giving it to the publisher. It is a work written to amuse the author. The pleasure of writing becomes an end in itself, a recreational pause after the rigors of law school. Poissenot's attention to the form of the preface masks a vagueness of purpose. He begins with the obligatory *sententia:* "Les vieux ont toujours ce proverbe en la bouche que, si jeunesse sçavoit et vieillesse pouvoit, tout se porteroit bien au monde" [Old men are constantly repeating that if youth knew how and old age could, all would be well with the world] (*L'Esté:* p. 52). The proverb serves to explain the cause of the singular indirection and lack of success which have led him to write—his youth. He writes to pick up his spirits—already boosted by the good weather. He leaves us to conjecture that the act of writing is a gratuitous act, since the weather might have worked its magic without the writing enterprise. What remains is the picture of a work told in summer, written in summer, a work badly structured ["mal fagotté"], prematurely published at the encouragement of a well-meaning friend. Poissenot's statement of intention is more a retrospection on a frivolous, youthful gesture than the deliberate act of recording and preserving for posterity proposed by the preface to Yver's *Printemps,* the authoritative source on which Poissenot claims to model his work.

The gifted prologuist—and we have cited many in the present study—combines many functions: the genesis of the work, the choice of public, declared intention, among others, to launch the work.[44] It is a game, where chance and order cooperate to form neither an afterthought nor a foreword to be skipped over or forgotten, but an integral part of the process of literary production.

5
Bridging the Gap:
The Transition to the Main Text

As the function of the prologue grows in importance in the course of the Renaissance, the *préfacier* becomes increasingly conscious of the problematic role of the preface. How can an author predict the reaction of a public whose tastes are constantly changing? The desire to set up a "good reading" of the text is accompanied by a growing awareness that interpretation lies at least partially beyond the province of the author.

Elizabeth Eisenstein, in her seminal work on printing, clearly demonstrates just how changes in book format bring about changes in thought patterns.[1] Guiding the reception and interpretation of the text is further complicated by the rapid growth in book production. The social, intellectual, and religious diversity of the reading public served to undermine any attempt to reduce a text to a single interpretation. We have seen in the previous chapter that the more Renaissance storytellers expand their prologues, the more they express skepticism about achieving the conventional goals of the prologue: explaining the generating circumstances of the work, providing a preview or summary of the work, preparing the reader for what is to come, warding off potential criticism, to name but a few.

Comments on the writing of prologues—what we shall refer to here as metacommentary—do more to focus on the *discours d'escorte* or companion discourse than on the main text which it is supposed to introduce. Such metacommentary can be said to widen instead of bridging the gap between liminary and principal discourse, a function conventionally assigned to the preface. The pages to follow are devoted to an analysis of the techniques used by the *conteurs* to ease the transition between prefatory comments and the work itself.

Bridging the gap is not a function mentioned in Genette's exhaustive list of prefatory functions, and yet it is essential in guiding the reception of the text to follow. The formal role played by the *cornice* comes to mind in setting up the artistic rules guiding the narrative. A frame set up within the prologue tends to separate the historic circumstances in which the work was created from the narrative space of the main text. Guido Almansi tells us that the *cornice* of the *Decameron*, presented in the introduction to the first day, "invites us to take part in an artistic game with fixed rules, while at the same time it forces the reader to be continuously aware of the fact of its being literature, part of the genre of storytelling."[2] It is an estranging device, "an *oestranenye*," a term introduced by the Russian formalists.[3]

Anticipating the narrative world in the main text, the prologue in the form of *cornice* performs a very different function from those carried out by the prologue dealing with the circumstances of the book's composition and production. The distinction is so obvious that we propose creating two categories to class the various types of prologues. In the first category, the prologue calls attention to the publication of the book. Virtually all of Genette's functions pertaining to the original prologue fall under this macro-function. In the second category, the prologue sets up a narrative screen to distance the historic world in which the book appears from the artistic world of the fictional work. The storytellers or *devisants* act as intermediaries between the author and the reader to guide the artistic interpretation of the text. We remember that the *Decameron*, both in the original and in the Le Maçon translation—as distinct from the translation by Laurent de Premierfait—includes both types of prologues: the *proemio* recounting the themes of how and why the author had composed the work, and the introduction to the first day, recounting the plague—the inhospitable historic climate. The horror of pestilence demands a creative response in which the "gay company" [*la brigata*] can find relief in art: "the *cornice* in the *Decameron* comes to fulfill two parallel functions: first it vouches for the artistic nature of everything that goes on within it by reminding the reader/spectator that the framed object must be considered according to artistic experience; second, it maintains the necessary distance (cerebral, visual, temporal) between the world of the fable and the lived, everyday world . . . the *vécu*."[4]

As the *cornice* comes to us in French literature, it is sometimes classed as prologue (*L'Heptaméron*), or more frequently, constitutes an introduction to the main text, as we see in the *Propos rustiques*, *Le Printemps*, and *Le Moyen de Parvenir*. In any case, such a frame unquestionably fulfills the liminary function of setting up a "good reading" of the text, in so much as the storytellers act as screens in "preventing too close and dangerous contact between the *text* and the act of reading it."[5] Should readers find fault with an episode based on the lack of verisimilitude, the storytellers are there to remind them of the artistic ends—whether playful or serious—of the narrator.

The categories defined above are in a sense antithetical and work against each other. How does one call attention to the historic event surrounding the appearance of the work and at the same time define the entrance to the fictional world? The dilemma explains in part why a prologue whose primary objective centers on the appearance of the work sometimes fails to create a smooth transition into the artistic world it introduces. The liminary apparatus of the early *conteurs* discussed in the present study, the anonymous author of the Burgundian *Cent Nouvelles Nouvelles* and Philippe de Vigneulles, focus on the historic and social circumstances surrounding the genesis of the work. While setting his own efforts within a strong narrative tradition, the author begins to take credit for the "regional" aspects of the tales to follow as well as for the errors and infelicitous turns of phrase. No transitional introduction marks the abrupt shift from stylistic commentary on the tales to follow and the beginning of the first tale. Beyond references to the regional and thus authentic content of the tales, no ground rules have been set to guide the reception of the text. There is no screen, no mediating force to frame the tales as an identifiable artistic object. No estranging figure or device prevents that "too close and dangerous contact" between the text and the reading process of which Almansi speaks.[6] With the appearance of Rabelais's first works, *Pantagruel* and *Gargantua*, and of Des Périers' *Nouvelles Récréations et Joyeux Devis*, a single element advances the prologue's capacity to bridge the gap into the main text. When the tone of the prologue reflects the playful, exuberant tone of the main text, the liminary apparatus seems more an extension of the principal text than a separate entity. With Rabelais and Des Périers, the unity of tone guarantees the integration of the liminary pages into the narrative whole. Whether these authors are more successful *préfaciers* because of their innovations is not our concern here, but their innovations demand attention in a work devoted to prefatory strategy.

It is evident that both Rabelais and Des Périers sought to distinguish their prologues to narrative adventures from the prologues to scholarly translations or to philosophical works whose end was instructive rather than recreative. Tone and linguistic register were two means of making the distinction immediately apparent in the opening paragraph of the prologue. Yet having resolved this problem, they were not ready or willing to abandon other prefatory practices, such as commentary on the historical, social, and intellectual content of the work, claims for the entertainment value of the work (Des Périers and Rabelais), or claims for its intellectual value (Rabelais), and finally, disparaging comments to potential critics.

As early as his first book, *Pantagruel*, Rabelais provides a means of leading into the narration from the prologue and of linking the opening paragraph of the main text to the concluding lines of the prologue. Breaking off a string of insults addressed to the skeptics among his readers, Alcofrybas concludes the prologue with a transitional phrase inviting us into the narrative: "et comme Sodome et Gomorre puissiez tomber en soulphre, en feu et en abysme, en cas que vous ne croyez fermement tout ce que je vous racompteray en ceste presente *Chronicque!*" (*Oeuvres complètes*, I: p. 219); [and like Sodom and Gomorrah may you dissolve into sulphur, fire, and the bottomless pit, in case you do not firmly believe everything that I tell you in the present Chronicle] (*Gargantua & Pantagruel:* p. 169). The word *chronicque* modulates the transition to the narrative, for all chronicles can be traced to a generating source—in the present case, the birth of Pantagruel, which Alcofrybas cleverly links to the chronicles of the "bons hystoriographes" of Antiquity: "car je voy que tous bons hystoriographes ainsi ont traicté leurs Chronicques, non seullement les Arabes, Barbares et Latins, mais aussi Gregoys, Gentilz, qui furent buveurs eternelz (*Oeuvres complètes*, I: p. 221); [For I observe that all good historiographers have thus dealt with their chronicles, not only the Arabs, Barbarians, and Romans, but also the gentile Greeks, who were everlasting boozers] (*Gargantus & Pantagruel:* p. 171). The reference to *buveurs*, which, unlike *verolez*, has not yet made its way to the prefatory discourse, is not far removed. It assumes its rightful place at the outset of the prologue to *Gargantua*. An even more cordial invitation bids us to move from the prologue of *Gargantua* to the main text: "Or esbaudissez vous, mes amours, et guayement lisez le reste, tout à l'aise du corps et au profit des reins! Mais escoutez, vietz d'azes,—que le maulubec vous trousque!—vous soubvienne de boyre à my pour la pareille, et je vous plegeray tout ares metys" (*Oeuvres complètes*, I: p. 9); [Now be cheerful, my dear boys, and read joyfully on for your bodily comfort and to the profit of your digestions—God rot you!—do not forget to drink my health for the favour, and I'll return you the toast, post-haste] (*Gargantua & Pantagruel:* p. 39). After completing the drier, more expository functions of the prologue: genesis, importance of the work, potential criticism, explanation of title and context, Alcofrybas leads us into the narrative with a sincere but familiar invitation more typical of spoken than written speech. In contrast to the *incipit* to the first chapter of *Pantagruel*, the opening line of *Gargantua* is linked not to the preceding prologue but to the previous work, thus providing retrospective publicity for the author's works: "Je vous remectz à la grande chronicque Pantagrueline recongnoistre la genealogie et antiquité dont nous est venu Gargantua" (*Oeuvres complètes*, I: p. 11); [For knowledge of the Gargantua's genealogy and of the antiquity of his descent, I refer you to the great Pantagrueline Chronicle] (*Gargantua & Pantagruel:* p. 41). The opening has a distinctly specular quality, as it mirrors the first chapter of *Pantagruel*, which in turn reflects the Biblical genealogies.[7]

With the *Tiers Livre*, the prologuist retains the invitational formula at the end of the prologue, but it no longer occupies the very last words of the *discours d'escorte*. The friendly invitation to his chosen readers has been relegated to the penultimate liminary space, and the final paragraph is a heated invective against his censors who approach the work with a biased attitude and disregard the rules he sets up for a good reading of the text: "moienant laquelle jamais en maulvaise partie ne prendront choses quelconques" (*Oeuvres complètes*, I: p. 401); [which means that they will never take in bad part anything] (*Gargantua & Pantagruel:* p. 286). It is indeed a bumpy ride from the spirited invective at the end of the prologue—"Jamais ne puissiez vous fianter que à sanglades d'estrivieres, jamais pisser que à l'estrapade, jamais eschauffer que à coups de baston!" (p. 403); [May you never manage a shit without being lashed with stirrup leathers, may you never squeeze out a piddle without being strappadoed, and may your body never be warmed except by a good hiding!] (p. 287)—to the rather dry resumption of the tales of Pantagruel. As we have stated earlier, only the humorous statistics reveal the narrator's tongue in cheek attitude toward his chronicle: "Pantagruel, avoir entierement conquesté le pays de Dipsodie, en icelluy transporta une colonie de Utopiens en nombre de 9876543210 hommes" (p. 405); [After having completely conquered the land of Dipsodia, Pantagurel transported there a colony of Utopians to the number of 9876543210 men] (p. 289). In a curious reversal of roles, the prologue departs from the dull, expository style of many prefaces and adopts the colorful language of everyday speech, while the narrative, at least in its initial paragraph, parodies the painstaking attention to setting and detail characteristic of the "bons hystoriographes" mentioned at the outset of *Pantagruel*.

It is not until the *Quart Livre* that Rabelais resumes the smoother transitional mode of the earlier works. After a long narrative about which we will comment later, the prologuist invites his chosen readership, his gouty friends, to drink and listen: "Or, en bonne santé toussez un bon coup, beuvez en trois, secouez dehait vos aureilles, et vous oyrez dire merveilles du noble et bon Pantagruel" (*Oeuvres complètes* II: p. 29); [So there, since you are in good health, give a good cough for me, toss off three bumpers, give your ears a good shake, and you shall hear marvels of the noble and excellent Pantagruel] (*Gargantua & Pantagruel:* p. 449). Gone are the choppy invectives against his critics and censors, and we are again, once settled down and attentive, drawn into the first chapter. In spite of the roundabout means of stating the date ("On moys de juin, au jour des festes Vestales" *Oeuvres complètes* II: 31; [In the month of June, on the day of Vesta's feast] (*Gargantua & Pantagruel*, p. 451), obvious only to those with a good knowledge of Roman history and the works of Ovid, the narrator sets us at once on familiar ground with the congregation of his principal characters. Again, he creates a retrospective of the previous works by citing all the players. Rabelais has rediscovered the art of the smooth transition—the gap eased and bridged by the modulating presence of the "noble et bon Pantagruel."

We have noted elsewhere in the present study that as Rabelais's prologues evolve, exposition gradually makes way for narration. As the place given to narration in the prologue increases, the prologue becomes a kind of sample [échantillon] of the work to follow. The story of Couillatris, amusingly adapted from Aesop and transposed to the region around Chinon, occupies two-thirds of the prefatory space, twelve out of eighteen pages in the Jourda edition. The lively tone and brisk pace of the prologue sample gives the reader a basis for deciding whether or not to continue reading the main text. We can only guess that Rabelais chooses adapted stories rather than original episodes for the preface in order to start the reader off on familiar—not to mention culturally acknowledged "literary"—ground.

The importance given to the prologues in the critical analysis of Rabelais's work is an indication that the liminary apparatus plays a role distinct from that of the main text within the Rabelaisian *corpus*.

5: BRIDGING THE GAP

Between the *récits* included in his prologues and the commencement of the chronicles, there is always a return to prefatory discourse, whether in the form of an invitation to read or a string of abusive remarks aimed at his detractors. Preface and chronicle are distinct but interdependent units.

Not so with Rabelais's contemporary, Bonaventure Des Périers. His work begins not with a prologue, but with a first tale in the form of a preamble ("en forme de préambule"). The heading blurs the line between narration and liminary discourse, although, as we have seen, his preamble incorporates many prefatory functions.

What is innovative in his technique of bridging the gap is his decision to defy a convention already established before the advent of printing and then expanded with the new emphasis on the liminary apparatus by the great printers: Aldus in Italy, Estienne and de Tournes in France.[8] Des Périers's prologue will not be freestanding, but integrated into the first novella. Even more ingenious is his clever manner of creating a character whose name (*le plaisantin*—the joker) and actions illustrate the prevailing tone of the *Nouvelles Récréations*. Having told us that he writes not to instruct or moralize but to bring rejoicing and laughter to his public, the narrator, we recall, introduces the main character with a rhetorical figure: "Je loueroys beaucoup plus celuy de nostre temps, qui, . . . par une antonomasia, on l'ha appellé le plaisantin" [I would praise all the more our contemporary, whom, . . . by antonomasia, they called the joker] (*Les Nouvelles Récréations:* p. 18). A brief description of the dying man resting near the fire gives way to a rapid exchange between the sick man and the priest, reduced to silence by the witty retorts of the joker. Narration proves far more effective than exposition in putting the reader in the right frame of mind to read through the work.

The *plaisantin* anecdote serves to engage Des Périers's readers in the prologue and to secure, as a consequence, their commitment to the volume. Turning his back on conventional prefatory strategy, he catches the readers unaware and pushes them on to the second tale. Aside from a brief question from the narrator, "Que voulez vous de plus naif que cela? quelle plus grande félicité?" [What could you ask for more naïve than that, what greater bliss?], no screen of *devisants* mediates between the text and the reader. When the prologuist counsels his female readers to read heartily ("Lisez hardiment, dame et demoyselles : il n'y ha rien qui ne soit honneste" [Read on boldly, ladies and young ladies; there is nothing ignoble], he expressly invites such close interaction between text and reader (*Nouvelles Récréations:* p. 17).

The rather easy, conversational contact which Des Périers establishes with the reader contrasts sharply with the more rigid and controlled contact between Montaigne and his reader. The latter's notice to the reader has a distinctly liminary quality—in the etymological sense of the word *limen*, an architectural entry or threshold. The legal implication of "livre de bonne foy" [book of good faith] creates from the outset a cautious, formal, indeed rather distant tone with a decisive, admonitory ring: "Il t'advertit dès l'entrée, que je ne m'y suis proposé aucune fin, que domestique et privée" (*Essais*, 9; 2); [It warns you from the outset that in it I have set myself no goal but a domestic and private one]. Montaigne's *entrée* evokes that solid, stone barrier separating the public from the private self. Was not the tower in which he read and wrote a symbol of this separation? Finally, the brevity of his address to the reader, with its precise geographic and historic indications, leaves the impression that it could indeed have been carved in wood or stone. The fact that Montaigne made almost no changes in his liminary message, in spite of countless changes and additions made throughout the *Essais*, adds to this impression. Neil M. Larkin argues convincingly that the "Au lecteur" and the dedications of specific essays to particular friends and associates perpetuate the promise in the "Au lecteur" that he was writing for a small circle of people who already knew him.[9] Addressing his efforts to relatives and friends—to those who had learned to accept him and who could be expected to receive the *Essais* with some indulgence—was without a doubt a less intimidating experience than offering his book to the general public.

The closing of Montaigne's address to the reader appears to cut off transitional possibilities from the *avis* to the first essay. The final ring of "A Dieu donq' [So farewell], coupled with the earlier suggestion that his death will not be long in coming ["bien tost"], contributes to the solemn, formal tone of the passage. Instead of the conversational formulae of Des Périers's *préambule*, Montaigne recreates epistolary style: formal closure, place of composition, and date. In contrast to Rabelais's prologues, there is an element in the "Au lecteur" which does not invite response from the reader. Not a single rhetorical question of the type Rabelais and Des Périers sprinkle throughout their prologues suggests authorial concern for our thoughts and reactions.

Montaigne takes another tack in trying to secure the reader's attention and to pull him into the main text. Bridging the gap is accomplished not through linking the final sentence of the preface to the *incipit* of the first essay, but by planting within the liminary space the seeds of ideas which will bear fruit later on in the *Essais*. Claude Blum shows how the initial theme of the *avis*—the fact that Montaigne writes for family and friends—is developed and expanded to include a neighbor ["voisin"] (II, xviii, 647; 503), the world ["le monde"] (III, ix, 941; 736), and the people ["le peuple"] (III, ii, 782; 611; III, ix, 959; 750), and finally, in the twelfth essay of the second book, to some good man ["quelque honneste homme"] who will come to know the author through his book.[10] We have commented elsewhere on the embedding of the painting metaphor at significant moments of the text, first in the notice to the reader and in the preamble to the essay on friendship—critical for its content and for its placement midway in the first book.[11] The artistic endeavor of the "other self"—the friend—will momentarily replace or displace the self-portrait. That the promised displacement never occurs is not our concern here. Self-portraiture and the need to obey culturally dictated laws of *convenance* lead into the new world theme, "ces nations qu'on dict vivre encore sous la douce liberté des premieres loix de nature" [those nations which are said to live still in the sweet freedom of nature's laws] (*Essais*, 9: 2). At the outset of his work, Montaigne reveals his interest in the Indians of South America, a topic he develops fully in "Des Cannibales" (I, xxxi). In short, Montaigne's liminary discourse does not presume to reduce the lengthy work to a summary, but he uses the space to suggest what is to follow in a provocative way.

If Montaigne takes pains in this first address to the reader to conceal or smooth over any dividing line between his person and his book ("Ainsi, lecteur, je suis moy-mesmes la matiere de mon livre" [Thus, reader, I am myself the matter of my book] *Essais*, 9: 2), between experience as lived and as recorded in literary form, his precursors, contemporaries, and imitators are careful to mark the distinction between experiential reality and its artistic representation.[12] Almansi describes the Italian *cornice* as a "standard picture frame, i.e. a reminder that what is inside is an artistic object."[13] Within this screen "protecting the frontiers of narrative experience," the prologuist outlines the rules governing the artistic experience.

From Chapter Two of the present study we recall that in many collections of tales beginning with the Burgundian *Cent Nouvelles Nouvelles*, the prologuist often criticized material of exotic or erudite origin. The frame, on the other hand, marks the aesthetic quality of the work to follow as distinct from the events of contemporary daily life. Rules for drawing such distinctions are set forth in the prologue. In the *Heptaméron*, instead of devising an activity of her own invention, Parlamente opts for the more secure path of established literary convention, Boccaccio's *cornice*, the gathering of ladies and gentlemen of high birth, the lush description of the setting where the *devisants* will gather. The authority of her literary precursors, whose artistry has won the approval of the royal family, outweighs her desire to innovate. Invention, either on the part of the teller or the listener, leads to artifice and deceit. Truth as a single overriding aesthetic guideline ["la verité de l'histoire"] will govern both literary production and literary reception within the artistic frame which separates the events of the *Heptaméron* from the events of daily life (*L'Heptaméron:* p. 9). The frame acts to screen the personal interpretive bias of the reader, as the commentary of various *devisants* guides but rarely dictates the interpretation of the tales.

The screen through which we are to view Du Fail's *Propos rustiques* accents the superior wisdom of the village elders, wisdom grounded in common sense and long experience (*Conteurs français du XVIe*: p. 607). Whether, as Gabriel A. Pérouse suggests, Du Fail begins with a somewhat facetious intention to poke fun at the elders, the affection with which he describes them and his attention to detail contributes to a lively, sympathetic portrait of the elders.[14] To the sixteenth century reader tossed about in a sea of uncertainties, where conflicting scientific and religious ideas provoke apprehension and civil unrest, the peaceful portrait of a homogeneous social group bound together by shared, unchanging values provides temporary relief from the strife of daily life.

In the opening to Jacques Yver's *Printemps*, the author takes pains to establish the contrast between the vicissitudes caused by the religious wars and the familiar, reassuring ground provided by an allegorical literary frame. The shift to allegory marks the passage to artistic endeavor. Once the historic circumstances in which the text was generated have been recounted, the frame functions to distance the narrative experience from the brutal and unpredictable events of history.

Built by the fairy Mélusine, the *château de Lusignan* is a triumph of artistry and artifice. The impeccable moral stature of the gentlemen of Bel-Accueil, Fleur d'Amour, and Ferme-Foy, names evoking the medieval romances, is rivaled only by the divine perfection of the two hostesses, Marie and Marguerite.[15] Even when expressly evoked, the civil strife seems far removed from the exquisitely framed portrait of refined pastimes.

In contrast to Yver's reassuring use of the *cornice* to describe the pleasures of country life in the leisured class, Béroalde de Verville's frame raises false expectations of order. Hints that we may indeed be taking part in a symposium accumulate in the early pages of the text. When at last the participants enter the banquet hall "Nous fusmes introduits en une belle grande sale paree . . . ." [We were introduced into a beautiful, richly-decorated great hall], we are introduced to such an array of literary figures that we can neither keep track of them nor make sense of their various roles in the work (*Le Moyen de Parvenir:* p. 5). The frame is a false promise of controlled artistic space, which under ordinary conditions would structure the text. But as in the misleading chapter headings, reflecting written rather than oral forms but arranged in a totally random order, Béroalde plays on our familiarity with recognizable literary forms, and then proceeds to distort their conventional usage to fit his own ludic intentions.[16] In a work whose liminary space is hardly recognizable from the main text, where the "pause dernière" [final pause] and "conclusion" appear in the early pages of the work, bridging the gap takes on new meaning. The gap refers not to the space between the liminary apparatus and the main text, but between the conventional notion of how the book should look and the subversion of this "look" by a playful author.

If the introductory pages of Béroalde's work fail to set up a "good reading" of the text—an impossible task when the text resists any sort of interpretation—these first pages do prepare the reader for what is to follow. Béroalde's opening is a kind of "mise en jeu sans prélude" [a putting into play and at stake without prelude], where all attempts to pin down specific and sustained meaning are doomed to failure.[17] To join in the game, the reader soon learns to subordinate all other rules to the aspect of play.[18] The misleading use of the frame breeds in turn in the reader a healthy skepticism for literary convention. As Gerald Prince observes, there never was, is not now, nor ever will be any plain, clear speech.[19] Faced with the multitude of functions assigned to the prologue, Béroalde blurs the distinction between preface and main text. The preface at once embraces the book and is embraced by it. With the *Moyen de Parvenir*, the prologue is literally everywhere.[20] Word and foreword belong to the same act of dissemination. For Béroalde, as for Montaigne, once the author has mortgaged his work to the public, he gives up control of its reception.

6
Women Addressing Women—The Differentiated Text

Although Renaissance practitioners of the short narrative form share many liminary strategies, some departures from common practice merit closer examination. Shunning the more current prefatory forms—the prologue and the *avis au lecteur,* Jeanne Flore, Hélisenne de Crenne, and Louise Labé show a predilection for the dedicatory epistle addressed sometimes to a single woman: "à madame Minerve sa chère cousine" [to Madame Minerva her dear cousin] (Flore, *Les Contes Amoureux*) or "à M.C.D.B.L." ("à Mademoiselle Clémence de Bourges lionnoize" [to Miss Clémence de Bourges Lyonnaise]) (Labé, *Le Débat de Folie et d'Amour*), or to a collectivity of women: "à toutes honestes Dames" [to all honorable ladies] (Hélisenne de Crenne, *Les Angoisses douloureuses qui procedent d'amours*).[1]

Addresses to clearly defined social groups, such as Bouchet's prefatory remarks to the merchants of Poitiers in the *Serées* (1584) are rare among the Renaissance *conteurs*. Rabelais's readers may choose to include or exclude themselves from the ranks of the *beuveurs/ verolez* [boozers/poxy ones]. He progressively widens the circle of *destinataires* in his prologues from the "chevaleureux champions, gentilz hommes et aultres" [chivalrous champions, gentlemen and others] he addresses in *Pantagruel* to the *beuveurs/verolez/goutteux* [boozers/poxy ones/gouty ones] of *Gargantua* and the *Tiers Livre*, and finally, the "gens de bien" [good people] of the *Quart Livre*. Des Périers and Marguerite de Navarre address their readers in the genderless you [*vous*], with Des Périers calling upon the ladies to read boldly on or to let their brothers and cousins censor the off-color material ["passages trop gaillars"].[2] He extends readership to include both sexes, sometimes evoked in the masculine ("mon amy" [my friend] p. 14), sometimes in the feminine ("Lisez hardiment, dames et demoyselles" [Read on boldly, Ladies and young ladies,] *Nouvelles Récréations:* p. 17), and to the young and the more mature ("entre vous femmes"/"entre vous fillettes" [among you women/among you girls], p. 17). Likewise in the *Heptameron*, gender parity among the inscribed storytellers—five men and five women—and among the historic figures mentioned in the prolgoue, "le roy François, premier de ce nom, monseigneur le Daulphin, madame la Daulphine, madame Marguerite" [King Francis, the first of this name, Monseigneur the Dauphin, Madame the Dauphine, and Madame Marguerite], implies that the sparing *vous* with which the narrator addresses the reader includes readers of both sexes.[3] Philippe de Vigneulles ends his prologue by begging "tous ceulx et celles" [all those men and ladies] who read his tales to take the good that is in them and to correct the flaws.[4]

Many *conteurs* choose the gender-distinct form "au lecteur" [to the reader] or "aux lecteurs"/"aux liseurs" [to the readers] to address their readers. We cite Noël du Fail, Philippe d'Alcripe, Cholières, La Motte-Messemé in this regard.[5] But is the address "au lecteur" really a gender distinct form? A case can be made, as Monique Wittig does with the pronoun subject *ils* [they], for assuming that the masculine form "au lecteur" or "aux lecteurs" does not exclude women, but that it is simply an *unmarked* form to address a general readership.[6] In contrast, the feminine form "aux lisantes" [to women readers], used by Hélisenne de Crenne in the liminary dixain preceding her dedicatory epistle to the *Angoisses douloureuses*, is a *marked* form set apart for two reasons: first, because of the infrequency of its usage in the prefatory discourse of Renaissance storytellers, and secondly, because in French a feminine form is never the "bearer of a universal point of view."[7] Similarly, Jeanne Flore's *Contes amoureux* begin with a poem addressed by madame Minerve to the "Nobles Dames amoureuses" [Noble Ladies in Love].[8] Louise Labé follows in the tradition of narrating to a feminine audience in her *Débat de Folie et d'Amour*. She addresses her prefatory remarks to a woman, Clémence de Bourges, and her use of personal pronouns suggests that she is speaking to an exclusively feminine audience. Such a one to one exchange between "dames lionnoises" [Lyonnaise ladies] as François Rigolot and Kirk D. Read remark, signals a common front—a community of interests.[9]

Labé's dedicatory epistle is an appeal to women not only to take up studies and writing—areas from which she had formerly been excluded by the stern laws of men ["severes loix des hommes"], but in knowledge and eminence to surpass or equal men: ["mais en science et vertu passer ou egaler les homes"] (*Débat*, 18, ll. 25–26, Wilson, p. 148). The preface opens by highlighting exclusion on the basis of gender: "Estant le tems venu, Mademoiselle, que les severes loix des hommes n'empeschent plus les femmes de s'apliquer aus sciences et disciplines" [The time having come, Mademoiselle, that the stern laws of men no longer bar women from devoting themselves to the sciences and disciplines] (*Débat*, 17, ll.1–3; Wilson, p. 148). On the one hand, she urges women to take up letters to show men the harm they have done to women by excluding them:

> il me semble que celles qui ont la commodité, doivent employer cette honneste liberté que *notre* sexe ha autre fois tout desiree, à icelles aprendre : et montrer aus hommes le tort qu'*ils nous* faisoient en *nous* privant du bien et de l'honneur qui *nous* en pouvoit venir. (ll. 3–8, emphasis added)

> [it seems to me that those who are able ought to employ this honorable liberty, which our sex formerly had desired so much, in studying these things and show men the wrong that they have done us in depriving us of the benefit and honor which might come to us.] (Wilson: p. 148)

The reader notes with some irony that Labé's grammar is as exclusionary as the harsh law of men about which she is complaining. Systematically throughout the preface, she uses the first person plural *nous* [we/us] to embrace both her readers—those whom she is exhorting to action—and herself. The men, referred to either as "les hommes" or *ils* [they], are evoked but not addressed in her preface. Prefatory discourse, which in general practice during the French Renaissance tended toward inclusion rather than exclusion, is transformed into an instrument of exclusion on the basis of gender. Learning, as distinct from jewelry and sumptuous clothing, is not a gift from the patriarchy—fathers, suitors, and husbands—but once acquired, belongs to women: "Mais l'honneur que la science nous procurera, sera entierement notre" [But the honor which knowledge will bring to us will be entirely our own] (*Débat*, 17, ll. 13–15; translation mine).

Established at the outset of the preface, the bipolar opposition of *nous* [the community of women] and *ils* [the men] continues to function throughout. There is no reason why the second part of the preface, devoted to a discussion of the therapeutic value of writing, could not include common, non-gender specific experiences shared by all writers. But the appropriation of *nous* [we/us] and *notre* [our] by the

6: WOMEN ADDRESSING WOMEN—THE DIFFERENTIATED TEXT

female community of writers ensures the exclusion of the male writer and reader:

> Mais quand il avient que mettons par escrit nos concepcions, combien que puis après notre cerveau coure par une infinité d'afaires et incessament remue, si est ce que long tems après reprenans nos escrits, nous revenons au mesme point, et à la mesme disposicion où nous estions. (*Débat*, p. 19, ll. 61–67)

> [But when we put our thoughts into writing, even if afterwards our minds race through no end of distractions and are constantly agitated, nevertheless, returning much later to what we have written, we find ourselves at the same point and in the same state of mind we were in before.] (Wilson: p. 150)

In preferring the now gender specific *nous* to the indefinite, ungendered *on*, Labé relegates the male sex to the mute state previously experienced by women under the "severes loix des hommes." Once empowered—in poetics if not yet in legal matters—the female voice does not resist exclusionary grammatical practices.

The men whom Labé has barred from participating in her observations on the value of writing (ll. 38–82) make a surprise reappearance in the last lines of the preface. It is they who have encouraged her to publish her work: "Mais depuis *quelcuns* de mes amis ont trouvé moyen de les lire sans que j'en susse rien, et que . . . *ils* m'ont fait à croire que les devois mettre en lumiere" (ll. 82–86, emphasis added); [But since some of my friends found a way to read them without my knowing anything about it, and . . . since they have persuaded me that I should bring them to light] (Wilson: p. 150). Lest we interpret *quelcuns* [some, any] to include men and women, we have an example of *quelcune*, the feminine form, used earlier in the preface, when she speaks of some women achieving fame and honor in letters: "et si *quelcune* parvient en tel degré, que de pouvoir mettre ses concepcions par escrit, le faire songneusement et non dédaigner la gloire" (ll. 8–10); [And if any woman reaches the stage at which she is able to put her ideas into writing, she should do it with much thought and should not scorn glory] (Wilson: p. 149). The friends who urged her to publish are male friends.

In spite of her exclusionary poetics in reserving her prefatory remarks for women and excluding men from the community of writers and readers whom she is addressing, Labé claims that her own voice would have remained silent—or at least unpublished—had it not been for the encouragement of her male friends. "Mettre par escrit nos concepcions" [putting our thoughts into writing] is one thing, making them public is another, and for that she needed two things: first, the encouragement of her male friends, more used to venturing out alone in public, and then the presence of another woman as guide, since women do not go out alone in public of their own free will: "Et pource que les femmes ne se montrent volontiers en publiq seules, je vous ay choisie pour me servir de guide, vous dediant ce petit euvre" (ll. 88–91; [And because women do not willingly appear alone in public, I have chosen you to serve as my guide, dedicating this little work to you] (Wilson: p. 150). Clémence de Bourges serves the role of guide, and her reputation as a young woman of chaste morals ("jeune fille aux moeurs très pures") will help protect the reputation of the author of the *Débat de Folie et d'Amour*.[10]

Along with their expressed reluctance to address a large, mixed audience, another characteristic which marks the prologues of the *conteuses* mentioned above is a tendency to adhere more strictly to the Boccaccian model than we notice in the prefatory discourse of the *conteurs*. These two traits are in fact interrelated in that Boccaccio addresses his work, as we noted earlier, to the "graziosissime donne," the refined ladies who love ["quelle che amano"] and seek relief from their suffering (*Decameron, Opere*: p. 8; *The Decameron*: p. 3).

Boccaccio assumes the posture of a kind of agent of justice, writing to redress the unequal treatment of the female sex by Fortune, who was so stingy in meting our relief and support to women who are unhappy in love: "Adunque, acciò che per me in parte s'ammendi il peccato della Fortuna, la quale dove meno era di forza, si come noe nelle dilicate donne veggiamo, quivi piú avara fu di sostegno, in soccorso et rifugio de quelle che amano" [Therefore I wish to make it up in part for the wrong done by fortune, who is less generous in the support where there is less strength, as we witness in the case of our delicate ladies. As support and diversion for those ladies in love] (p. 8: p. 3). He describes himself as a champion of the weaker sex, confined by the wishes, whims, and commands of fathers, mothers, brothers, and husbands [ristrette da' voleri, da' piaceri, da' comandamenti de' padri, delle madri, de' fratelli e de' mariti]. In contrast to the harsh rule of the family, Boccaccio offers the delicate ladies entertainment and uplifting advice. Help comes from outside the restricted circuit of female discourse. Boccaccio's work is a lifeline held out to save the foundering women. That help could come from within

6: WOMEN ADDRESSING WOMEN—THE DIFFERENTIATED TEXT 95

the confined area of their rooms ["nel piccolo circuito delle loro camere"] does not occur to Boccaccio. Inspiration must be sparked from without—the confinement is synonymous with silence and suffering.[11]

In adapting Boccaccian prefatory strategies to their particular circumstances, Jeanne Flore, Hélisenne de Crenne, and Louise Labé find their inspiration from within the confines of feminine company. From Madame Minerve, to whom Jeanne Flore dedicates her prefatory remarks, to the feminine circle of cousins and friends ["cousines et amyes"] who are both tellers and listeners of the love tales told at the wine harvest, Jeanne Flore's narrative cadre is distinctly feminine. The allegorical names of the tellers—Madame Meduse, Madame Sapho, Madame Andromeda, Madame Cassandre—lend the weight of antiquity, but a distinctly feminine antiquity, to the *Contes amoureux*.

The impetus for writing down and publishing the tales does not extend beyond the pleasure and instruction of female readers. Unlike Boccaccio, Flore gives primacy to the pleasure factor: "Puis tout soubdain je me suis advisée que je feroys chose tres *agreable* et *plaisante* aux jeunes Dames amoureuses, lesquelles loyaulment continuent au vray service d'Amour, et lesquelles se *delectent* de lire telz *joyeulx* comptes, si je les faisois tout d'ung train gecter en impression" [Then suddenly I realized that I would do something very pleasant and agreeable for women in love who loyally persist in love's true service and who take joy in reading such merry tales, if I had them published at once] (*Contes Amoureux*, 97, ll. 14–17, emphasis added).

She makes but one reference to a wider range of readers, and it is in the context of an apology for her rough and disorganized style: "Neantmoins soubs espoir que vous, et les humains lecteurs excuserez le rude et mal agencé langaige. C'est oeuvre de femme, d'où ne peult sortir ouvraige si limé, que bien seroit d'ung homme discretz en ses escriptz" [Nevertheless, in the hope that you and other understanding readers will excuse the rough and poorly constructed language; it's the work of a woman out of which cannot come a work as polished as the writings of an unobtrusive man would be] (97, ll. 19–21). Going beyond the humility commonplace found in most prefaces, Flore expresses concern that once her tales reach the world outside the circle of women for whom and by whom they were conceived, they will meet with disapprobation. The outer circle of "humains lecteurs" is perhaps less humane and more critical. The *préfacière* is coming to grips with reader expectation, and here it is unquestionably the well fashioned [*limé*] discouse of male authors which sets the standards. Jeanne Flore is faced with what Hélène Cixous calls the "tourment de la venue à la parole," woman's distress at realizing that when she speaks, she commits a transgression. In so doing she suffers a double anguish, for while she speaks, she violates the order which have woman confined to silent listening, violates the expectations of the audience whose ear is attuned to the male voice.[12] Set against the discourse of "un homme discretz" [an unobtrusive male] the female voice is by extension "indiscreet."

Renaissance *conteurs* were not exempt from pre-publication jitters. Philippe de Vigneulles begs his readers to pardon his errors and to supply their own corrections.[13] What sets Flore's remarks apart is her statement that her discourse is marked by faulty structure and can be differentiated from that of "ung homme discretz en ses escriptz." Gender, as well as expectations established on the basis of gender, informs the reception of literary discourse.

Hélisenne makes no mention of potential male readers in her dedicatory epistle. She is specific in restricting her audience to the aristocracy: "C'est à vous, mes nobles Dames, que je veulx mes extremes doleurs estre communiquées. Car j'estime que mon infortune vous provocquera à quelques larmes piteuses: qui me pourra donner quelque refrigeration medicamente" (*Angoisses douloureuses*, éd. Secor, p. 3: ll. pp. 7–9); [it is to you, my noble ladies, that I wish to communicate my extreme sorrows. For I believe that my misfortune will draw from you pitying tears which will be a cooling medication to me] (Wilson: p. 197). Hélisenne places expectations on her readers, expectations again based on gender, and more specifically, the female capacity for compassion. Again, help is sought from within the closed group of female listeners and only from this group.

Marking her difference from Boccaccio, who writes to comfort others only after his love has lost its force ("il mio amore . . . per se medesimo in processo di tempo si diminuí," [my love . . . diminished by itself in the couse of time]) (*Decameron*, p. 7; p. 2), Hélisenne writes out of self-interest in the hopes that the tears and compassion of a sympathetic audience will chill her passion. Of secondary interest is her hope that the sight of her suffering will serve as a warning to other women, that they may avoid love's dangerous snares ["eviter les dangereux lacqs d'amour"] ll. 16–17).

Ending her epistle with an invocation to the Mother of Christ, "celle qui est mere et fille de l'altiltonant plasmateur" [her who is mother and daughter of the high thundering Creator], Hélisenne de

Crenne makes it clear that help can come only from within the closed network of communication among women. By replacing the classical muses with a Christian muse, Hélisenne is substituting one feminine source of inspiration for another (*Angoysses douloureuses*, 4, ll. 22–23). The weak hand ["debile main"] with which she writes must learn to write well ["bien escrire"] under the tutelage of the Virgin Mary. Her act of omission—her refusal to admit the male agents of her suffering onto the prefatory pages of her work—effectively silences the male voice and obstructs the flow of either understanding or criticism from the male sector. She passes over in silence the role of the male *auctor* as source, model, and inspiration, a role which neither of her contemporaries Jeanne Flore or Louise Labé fails to acknowledge. Refusing an audience whose expectations she might disappoint, Hélisenne prefers not to compete for time with a group more experienced than she in public discourse. Instead, she confines her audience to a group whose ear is attuned to a woman's halting efforts at self-expression.[14]

Hélisenne retains the dedicatory address to her female readership in the second part of the *Angoysses*, dedicated to all noble and virtuous ladies ["à toutes nobles et vertueuses dames"]. It becomes clear, however, that she envisions—but does not directly address—another audience made up of modern gentlemen ["les gentilz hommes modernes"] who might be inspired to pursue "martial exercise" by the example of her *amy* Guenelec, whose voice she will assume (Angoysses, *Seconde Partie*, p. 147, l. 25). Preparing herself to speak in his voice, she evokes, as she had not in the initial dedicatory epistle, the ultimate male *auctor*, Homer, and the authority of the *Iliad* in inspiring Alexander to virtuous action. She hopes that her little book ["petit livre"] will have the same effect. If Guenelec was importunate in pursuing his lady, his virtue should not be called into question, but rather the essence of the male sex, "car telle est l'humaine virile condition que durant le temps qu'ils n'ont encours jouy de la chose aymée, ilz ne pardonnent à aulcuns perilz puis que c'est pour parvenir d'avoir de leurs desirs contentement, comme vous aultres jeunes hommes le scavez" [for such is men's natural bent that as long as they have not yet possessed the beloved, they spare no danger in seeking the satisfaction of their desires, as you other young men know] (149, ll. 87–92). At the very moment she attacks a major flaw in the male character, she expands her readership to include the young male reader in her prefatory remarks.

The third part of the *Angoysses* immediately includes the men among her readers. In the previous book, addressed to the noble and virtuous ladies, the narrator had changed the opening address from benevolent readers ["lecteurs benevoles"] to read my benevolent ladies ["mes dames benevoles"] and so opted for a gender specific form of address (*Angoysses douloureuses*, 146, l. 1, note). In the third book, she retains the inclusive noble readers ["nobles lecteurs"], but, as in the example above, inclusion has its price—criticism of man's character. Adam, not Eve, was responsible for man's fall from Grace: "Car si le premier homme n'eust esté ingrat envers celluy qui est autheur de tout—duquel il avoit reçeu tant de benefices—il ne fust succumbé en la mortelle ruyne pecheresse dont en sont contaminez tous ses posterieurs" [For if the first man had not been ungrateful to him who is the author of all things—from whom he had received so many blessings—he would not have given in to the fatal, sinful ruin by which all his descendants are tainted] (ll. 4–8).

The narrative voice of the third book aspires to loftier goals than the pursuit of martial arts. To help reinforce her plea to men to resist their second nature, she evokes the authority of Saint Paul—that apostle so often cited by men to criticize the inconstant nature of woman's virtue: "La chair et concupiscence est adversaire de l'esperit; et l'esperit es adversaire de la chair" [Flesh and lust are the enemy of the mind; and the mind is the enemy of the flesh] (ll. pp. 34–36). Hélisenne's rhetorical trick is to appropriate the mind for women: "mais qui sera ce, qui donnera port et faveur à l'esperit si ce n'est dame raison" [but who will be the one to give bearing and favor to the mind if not Lady Reason?] (ll. 36–37). Intellect, so long the province of men, as we see in Labé's preface, is here placed squarely in the female domain of Lady Reason. Sensuality is left as a male problem to be overcome through the reading of the *Angoysses* and with the tutelage of Dame Raison: "Parquoy, je vous obsecre que d'elle ne vous distinguez auculnement affin que par elle la sensualité succumbe et soit domptée" [Wherein I implore you not to distance yourself from her, so that by her, sensuality may give way and be overcome] (ll. 40–42). The *préfacière* has reversed the customary equation man = head, woman = body.

Of the four most noteworthy women writers of the first half of the sixteenth century, only Marguerite de Navarre breaks with the other women storytellers in insisting upon, in the first instance, an audience which includes both sexes. She, in a more explicit manner than Jeanne Flore, Hélisenne de Crenne, and Louise Labé, acknowledges her source of literary inspiration—Boccaccio and his *Decameron*—but rejects his address to an exclusively female audience. As stated earlier, the *je* who addresses the reader resists calling attention to the gender of either the sender or the receiver of the prologue. The unmarked voice of the primary narrator unveils the narrative frame with singular objectivity. The emotional suffering of the narrator, such an integral part of the prologues of Boccaccio and Hélisenne de Crenne, plays no role. If gender remains unmarked at the primary level, a fact which reinforces Philippe de Lajarte's notion of the transcendental character of the first narrative instance in the *Heptaméron*, gender assumes a prominent role at the fictional level of the frame.[15] Hircan clearly delineates the difference between male physical activities—the hunt—and female activities: handwork and dancing. Gender difference creates problems in choosing a common activity, as evidenced when Parlamente blushes as Hircan mentions his preferred pastime. It is in fact through dialogue that agreement is reached in spite of evident differences in personality. We are far from the confined space of a uniquely feminine community, and attitudinal differences enrich the dialogue.

Within the fictional frame of the *Heptaméron*, efforts are made by the storytellers to respect everyone's right to speak. Hircan's comment at the outset that at play, we (all men and women) are equal, "au jeu nous sommes tous égaulx," sets the tone (*L'Heptaméron:* p. 10). The storytellers alternate spinning tales on the basis of gender. When Saffredent fears that parity between the sexes has not been respected, he comments: "Vous m'avez faict l'honneur d'avoir commencé deux Journées: il me semble que nous ferions tort aux dames, si une seulle n'en commençoit deux" [You have given me the honor of beginning two days, and it seems to me that we would be committing an injustice towards the ladies if even one of them did not in turn begin two] (p. 421).

Equal right to self-expression is thus foregrounded in the frame of the *Heptaméron*. Repeated reference to respecting woman's right to speak, the parity of numbers of both sexes within the fictional and historic context, mention of doing injustice to women—these are signs of an authorial strategy to put men and women on an equal footing. Such a strategy is supported on the narrative level by the events of individual tales.[16]

Why does Marguerite de Navarre shun the female circle of discourse preferred by Jeanne Flore, Hélisenne de Crenne, and Louise

Labé in favor of a frame which establishes everyone's right to express an opinion? We noticed earlier that the primary narrator takes pains to avoid details which would call attention to the gender of either the sender or receiver of the prologue. We can only speculate that, unlike the other *conteuses*, Marguerite de Navarre is an empowered voice, used to speaking out and to being heard. Details within individual tales show the influence of the Queen of Navarre in intervening politically on behalf of people who, through no fault of their own, have run afoul of an unjust authority.[17]

It is fitting that her work should refuse the Boccaccian tradition of addressing a purely female audience.[18] Writing is presented as an activity open to participation and appreciation by both sexes, as evidenced by the narrator's mention that the *Decameron* was admired by Francis I, the Dauphin, his wife, and Marguerite herself (*L'Heptaméron:* p. 9). The historic effort by members of the court to generate a new work along the lines of Boccaccio's is not delineated along gender lines.

We can only conclude from her remarks that, for the Queen of Navarre, literary production is an open line of communication. Whether she perceived that by clearly excluding male readers at the outset of the work, women writers were marginalizing their literary efforts, we can only speculate. But by refusing to call attention to the gender of either the originator or the receiver of her discourse, by failing to mention woman's lack of skill or practice in writing for publication, Marguerite de Navarre inserts her work in the mainstream of sixteenth century literary discourse and secures for it a firm place among her fellow *conteurs*. In contrast, the works of her contemporary female *conteuses* are only beginning to emerge from the margins to which they had been relegated as a *discours de femme*. Had these women been speaking from the empowered position of the Queen of Navarre, they too may have used different prefatory strategies.

Afterword

From our examination of a variety of prologues to narrative works in the Renaissance, it is clear that these authors share a belief in the power of the preface to confer upon a text its status as book. To let the work venture forth without the *discours d'escorte* was to place its status in jeopardy. The same authors were equally aware of the shortcomings of liminary discourse. How could they, in such a limited space, ground their work firmly in the "authoritative sanction that external sources provide" and still preserve the integrity of their individual style and tone?[1] Some would try to accomplish both goals, while a few, like Des Périers, would neglect the authority of the source for the sake of setting forth ["avancer"] their individual voice. As we have seen, several women authors would seek to establish distinctions between their works and the works of the authoritative sources on the basis of gender. The women will at times subvert the liminary strategies used by their male counterparts, use the liminary space for criticism of the male character, or will substitute feminine authorities for the more common male literary figures within the prefatory space. In any case, both the male and female voice emerge as strong and individual in the prologues of the Renaissance.

In fact, it was the emergence of the singular voice of the author as distinct from the authoritative voices of the past that sets apart Renaissance texts from earlier works. Elizabeth Eisenstein speaks of "new forms of authorship and literary property" undermining "older concepts of collective authority."[2] As Barry Lydgate points out, the sometimes "idiosyncratic" self of the writer appeals to the sensitivities of a single "isolated reader" instead of to the collective participation evoked in medieval texts and even in the early Renaissance.[3] The examples of Noël du Fail and Montaigne and their address "au lecteur" come to mind.

In a recent work, Michel Jeanneret attributes the popularity of the banquet setting and "propos de table" to the Renaissance author's desire to attach literary phenomena to natural phenomena, to root literature in tangible reality.[4] Their privileging of the spoken over the written word was but one example of such a tendency.[5] Prefatory discourse—addressed to a second person in the form of the reader or readers—is the privileged space of direct discourse.

Eschewing for the most part the moralizing or didactic tone of the prefaces to both medieval and Renaissance theoretical texts or of translations of classical texts, our *préfaciers* use the liminary space to engage the reader in an animated discussion of contemporary issues: mention of contemporary events, concerns about the printing process, uneasiness about the reception of the text, fear of censorship or of writing to a hostile audience, and finally, a gradual recognition of the limitations of prefatory discourse.

On the threshold separating the historical world in which the text was written from the artistic space of the work, the preface prepares the reader to recognize the signs and rules which govern the artistic space. Liminary metaphors mark areas where the artistic world diverges from the more familiar world outside the work and serve to guide the newly initiated reader through this space. The readers emerge from the prologue better able to deal with the uncharted space before them.

As readers of Renaissance prefaces, we can understand the storyteller's impatience with the expositional parameters of the preface: dedication, introduction, descriptive summary, and advertisement. Spinning tales is their craft, not glossing or summarizing. As a consequence, narrative creeps naturally into the prologue and blurs the distinction between exposition and narration and between foreword an the narrative main text.

There is a distinct element of live, oral performance in the prologues of the Renaissance *conteurs*, what Zumthor refers to as a performing objective [visée performancielle"].[6] Traces of oral rather than written communication abound: the tendency to tack on elements instead of subordinating one thought to another, a preference for situational indices over abstract ideas, as well as the storyteller's call for the active participation of the reader by means of direct address or questions directed his way.

The *conteurs* and *conteuses* as writers of prefaces recall their ties to the medieval storytellers or, for that matter, with medieval preachers who knew that the best way to transmit information and implant it in the memory of the audience was to package it in narrative form. Rabelais's Couillatris, Des Périers's "joker," and Cholières's schoolboy are examples of narrative anecdotes used to illustrate an idea or concept. Reluctant to launch their works without a prologue, the storytellers opt for the preview—a sampling of narrative talent—in the way that the serial publication of their works served nineteenth century writers or film previews draw the crowds into modern theaters.

With the advent of the seventeenth century, the preface no longer narrates but anticipates or comments on the narrative to follow. It loses its narrative function. Perrault's preface to *Griseldis, Peau d'Ane,* and the *Souhaits ridicules,* although admittedly a late preface, furnishes no narrative sample, but situates the author's tales in relation to those of the ancients, those of his precursors, and those of his contemporaries. His primary design in the preface is not narration but the defense of the moral instruction contained within his work.[7] Apart from the first paragraph where subordinate clauses abound, elements of conversational and written discourse coexist. Yet the author proceeds to *tell* us how he views narrative instead of *showing* us a preview of his narrative talent. He respects the clear distinction between prefatory and narrative discourse. Prologues extending beyond their boundaries or seeking to destroy the artificial boundary between liminary and narrative text have little place in a period which strictly honors generic definitions.

The notion of the prologue as play "sans prélude," exemplified by so many Renaissance *conteurs,* could not survive the classical distaste for hybrid forms. We regret the shift, since the fusion or confusion of expository and narrative ends makes for better prefatory reading. If it has become common practice to slight prefatory statements in favor of the "main text," we may perhaps blame the seventeenth century insistence on generic purity.

Notes

Introduction

1. Gérard Genette, *Seuils* (Paris: Editions du Seuil, 1987), p. 7. Genette defines the paratext as "ce par quoi un texte se fait livre et propose comme tel à ses lecteurs, et plus généralement au public" [that by which a text becomes a book and offers itself as such to its readers, and more generally to the public]. He evokes such terms as *seuil* [threshold], vestibule, fringe, zone of transition and transaction to describe the critical placement of the paratext between the world outside and the world inside the book's cover. The title, table of contents, dedication, preface—either by the author or by another person, headings, notes, and even what he calls the *épitexte* (interviews, correspondence, etc.) constitute the paratext. See also the special issue of *Poétique* 69 (1987), and *Introduction à l'architexte* (Paris: Editions du Seuil, 1979), p. 80.

2. *L'Esprit Créateur* 27 (1987), p. 3.

3. *Versants* 15 (1989). The special issue is entitled *Prologues au XVI siècle*.

4. In *La Dissémination* (Paris: Editions du Seuil, 1972), Jacques Derrida discusses Hegel's attitude toward the preface as both superfluous, at least to philosophic discourse, and deceivingly reductive in all types of discourse. It is impossible to reduce a text to the effects of meaning, content, theme, or thesis that it creates, "Hors livre," pp. 13–15.

5. Tony Hunt, "The Rhetorical Background to the Arthurian Prologue: Tradition and the Old French Vernacular Prologues," *Forum for Modern Language Studies* 6, 1 (1972): pp. 320–344; A. J. Minnis, *Medieval Theory of Authorship. Scholastic Literary Attitudes in the later Middle Ages* (London: Scolar Press, 1984); Michel Zink, *La Subjectivité littéraire* (Paris: Presses Universitaires de France, 1985); Marie-Louise Ollier, "The Author in the Text: The Prologues of Chrétien de Troyes," *Yale French Studies* 51 (1974): pp. 26–41; Pierre-Yves Badel, "Rhétorique et Polémique dans les prologues de romans au Moyen Age," *Littérature* 20 (1975): pp. 81–93; and James A. Schultz, "Classical Rhetoric, Medieval Prologues, and the Medieval Vernacular Prologue," *Speculum* 59 (1984): pp. 1–15.

6. Estienne Tabourot, *Les Bigarrures du Seigneur des Accords*, edited by Guillaume Colletet (Geneva: Slatkine Reprints, 1969), I: p. 27 (I: p. 88 of the 1866 edition cited below). This is a facsimile edition of Guillaume Colletet's three-volume edition, *Les Bigarrures du seigneur des Accords avec les Apophthegmes du sieur Gaulard et les Escraignes dijonnaises*, 3 vols. (Bruxelles: A. Mertens et Fils, 1866). Colletet dates the original edition of the *Bigarrures* from 1583, I: p. 12 (p. 24 of the 1866 edition).

7. Michel de Montaigne, *Oeuvres complètes*, edited by Albert Thibaudet and Maurice Rat (Paris: Gallimard, 1962), p. 247. All translations of Montaigne's work are taken from *The Complete Essays of Montaigne*, translated by Donald M. Frame (Stanford, Calif.: Stanford University Press, 1976), pp. 186–187. For all citations from Montaigne's *Essais*, the first page number indicates the French edition and the second page number, the Frame translation.

8. Lucien Febvre and Henri-Jean Martin, *L'Apparition du livre* (Paris: Albin Michel, 1971), p. 126.

9. François Rigolot notes the role of deictics and modalizing expressions in the preface, such as here, now, this, that one, we, you, etc. The role of such expressions is to make the reader participate in the spatio-temporal universe of the text. See "Prolégomènes à une étude du statut de l'appareil liminaire des textes littéraires," *L'Esprit Créateur* 27, 3 (1987), pp. 7–18. Summing up J. L. Austin's *How to Do Things With Words*, edited by J. O. Urmson (London: Oxford University Press, 1962), Oswald Ducrot and Tzvetan Todorov distinguish performative utterances from constative utterances by the fact that a performative utterance can not be understood independently of the act it is trying to accomplish, *Dictionnaire encyclopédique des sciences du langage* (Paris: Editions du Seuil, 1972), pp. 428–29. When the prologuist asks for the attention of the reader, he both transmits a message ("Listen") and carries out a speech act—calling for attention.

10. Brunetto Latini, *Li Livres dou Tresor*, in *Collection de documents inédits sur l'histoire de France*, edited by P. Chabaille (Paris, Imprimerie impériale, 1863), vol. III, pp. 467–575.

11. Elizabeth L. Eisenstein, *The Printing Press as an Agent of Change*, Vol. 1 (Cambridge: Cambridge University Press, 1979), pp. 50–60.

12. Speaking about Montaigne, Hope Glidden addresses the problem of the author's uncertainty about his reading public: "The immediate problem is the mass public to which these essays go out—so diversified as to preclude any consensus over the meaning of words; a people so variegated in their literacy that classical tropes and borrowings would be lost on them," "Recouping the Text: The Theory and the Practice of Reading," *L'Esprit Créateur* 21, 2 (1981): pp. 25–37.

13. See Roger Dubuis, "La Genèse de la nouvelle en France au moyen âge," *Cahiers de l'Association des Etudes Françaises* 18 (1966): pp. 9–19.

14. *Les Cent Nouvelles Nouvelles*, in *Conteurs français du XVIe siècle*, edited by Pierre Jourda. Paris: Gallimard, 1956, p. 19.

15. Floyd Gray, *Rabelais et l'écriture* (Paris: A. G. Nizet, 1974); Dorothy Gabe Coleman, "The Prologues of Rabelais," *Modern Language Review*, 62, 3 (1967): pp. 407–19; François Rigolot, *Les Langages de Rabelais*. Etudes Rabelaisiennes X (Geneva: Droz, 1972); Gérard Defaux, "D'un problème l'autre: herméneutique de l'altior sensus' et 'captatio lectoris' dans le prologue de *Gargantua*," *Revue d'Histoire Littéraire de France* 2 (1985): pp. 196–216; Raymond La Charité, "Lecteurs et lectures dans le prologue de Gargantua," *French Forum* 10 (1985): pp. 261–70; Craig B. Brush, "Montaigne's Preface," *Teaching Language through Literature* 24, 2 (1985): pp. 27–36; Jean Starobinski, *Montaigne en mouvement* (Paris: Gallimard, 1982), pp. 44–49; Philippe de Lajarte, "Le Prologue de l'*Heptaméron* et le processus de production de l'oeuvre," in *La Nouvelle française à la Renaissance*, ed. Lionello Sozzi (Geneva: Slatkine, 1981), pp. 397–423; Gabriel A. Pérouse, "Le dessein des *Propos rustiques*," in *Etudes Seiziémistes offertes à Monsieur le Professeur V. L. Saulnier* (Geneva: Droz, 1980), pp. 137–50. The works listed represent only a small selection of studies devoted to the prologues of individual storytellers of the French Renaissance. Others will be mentioned throughout the present study.

16. J. Vianey, "Montaigne conteur," in *Mélanges de philologie et d'histoire littéraire offerts à Edmond Huguet* (Paris: 1940), p. 210; Hugo Friedrich, *Montaigne*, trans. R. Rovini (Paris: Gallimard, 1970), pp. 364–375.

17. Gabriel-A. Pérouse, "De Montaigne à Boccace et de Boccace à Montaigne," p. 15.

18. "Mr. de la Motte Messemé n'est point si riche, et, quand il veut se conformer

à Montaigne, il conte," [Mr. de la Motte Messemé is not so resourceful, and when he wants to follow Montaigne's model, he tells stories,] Pérouse, p. 18.

19. "Je nommerai ici *préface* . . . toute espèce de texte liminaire (préliminaire ou postliminaire), auctorial ou allographe, consistant en un discours produit à propos du texte qui suit ou qui précède," [I will call preface . . . any type of liminary text (preliminary or post-liminary), written by the author or by another, composed of a statement made up about the text which follows or precedes it,] *Seuils*, p. 150.

20. Manlio Cortelazzo and Paolo Zolli, *Dizionario etimologico della linqua italiana*, 5 vol. (Bologna: Zanichelli, 1985), 4: p. 967.

21. Dante Alighieri, *Epistole*, in *Tutte le opere*, ed. Luigi Blasucci (Florence: G. C. Sansoni, 1965), p. 346.

22. Giovanni Boccaccio, *Decameron*, in *Opere di Giovanni Boccaccio*, edited by Cesare Segre (Milan: U. Mursia, 1978), "Proemio," pp. 7–9. Translations, but not paraphrasing, refer to *The Decameron*, Trans. Mark Musa and Peter Bondanella (New York/London: W.W. Norton, 1982).

23. Tony Hunt, "The Rhetorical background to the Arthurian Prologue," p. 1. Speaking of Euripides, Hunt comments that the summarizing of ensuing narrative has remained one of the functions of literary prologues. In his *Annotationi nel libro della Poetica d'Aristotele* (1575), Piccolomini links the prologue to the theater: "il prologo primieramente s'intende esser quella parte tutta della tragedia, ch'innanzi al Parodo (o ver all'entrata del choro) è posta" [the prologue is mainly understood to be that entire part of the tragedy which is placed prior to the *parodos* (that is to say at the entrance of the chorus)] cited in the *Dizionario etimologica della lingua italiana*, 4: p. 882.

24. *Le Decameron de Messire Iehan Bocace Florentin, nouvellement traduict d'Italien par Maistre Anthoine le Maçon. . . . Imprimé à Paris pour Estienne Roffet dict le Faulcheur Libraire demeurant sur le pont sainct Michel à l'enseigne de la Roze blanche*. 1545.

25. *Les Bigarrures du Seigneur des Accords*, 28 or 92 of the 1866 edition. This edition is a facsimile of the 1866 edition by Colletet (Bruxelles: A. Mertens, 1866).

26. James Schultz notes that as far back as John of Garland, the *prooemium* was thought to aim at instruction, just as the *exordium* sought to persuade, "Classical Rhetoric, Medieval Poetics, and the Medieval Vernacular Prologue," p. 12.

Chapter 1. From *Auctor* to *Auteur*

1. Tony Hunt, "The Rhetorical Background to the Arthurian Prologue: Tradition and the Old French Vernacular Prologues," and A. J. Minnis, *Medieval Theory of Authorship. Scholastic Literary Attitudes in the later Middle Ages.*

2. Marie-Louise Ollier, "The Author in the Text: The Prologues of Chrétien de Troyes, Michel Zink, *La Subjectivité littéraire*, and James A. Schultz, "Classical Rhetoric, Medieval Prologues, and the Medieval Vernacular Prologue." I cite Schultz's remarks, p. 15.

3. Ollier, "The Author in the Text," p. 126.

4. Minnis, *Medieval Theory of Authorship*, p. 10.

5. Zink, *La Subjectivité littéraire*, pp. 32–35.

6. Ollier finds that while the term *conte* refers to the source or narrative sequence, *estoire* is used to guarantee "the authenticity of the narrative," its "credibility"—the source worthy of belief, "The Author in the Text," p. 28. We use appropriation in the sense defined by Weimann and best rendered by the German term *Aneignung*,

"making things one's own." "The German term has the advantage of not necessarily involving an ideologically preconceived idea of (private) ownership or (physical) property, instead it allows for acquisitive behavior . . . as well as the nonacquisitive acts of intellectual energy, possession, and assimilation," Robert Weimann, "Appropriation and Modern History in Renaissance Prose Narrative," *New Literary History* 14, 3 (1983): pp. 459-495. Concerning the increased authority granted because of the adapter's respect for his sources, Zink comments that the adapter's deference towards his sources only increases the stature and authority of the source, *La Subjectivité littéraire*, p. 35. We should at this point take note of Paul Zumthor's view that the term *mettre en roman* is not limited to a simple translation of the Latin source, but includes the concept of commentary and clarification that will make the work accessible to the public by adapting it to more contemporary contexts, *La Lettre et la voix* (Paris: Editions du Seuil, 1987), p. 301.

7. Discussed by Zink, *La Subjectivité littéraire*, 35. L. Constans, *Le Roman de Troie par Benoît de Sainte-Maure*, 6 vol. (Paris: S.A.T.F., 1904-1912), vv. 129-137.

8. Zink, *La Subjectivité littéraire*, pp. 38-39: "Tant con durra crestïantez." *Erec et Enide*, edited by Mario Roques (Paris: Champion, 1963), v. 26.

9. Ollier speaks of the remarkable play of tenses in Chrétien's prologues with the narrative present organizing the past and the future around itself, p. 36.

10. Minnis, p. 196: "whereas an *auctor* was regarded as someone whose works had considerable authority and who bore full responsibility for what he had written, the *compilator* firmly denied any personal authority and accepted responsibility only for the manner in which he had arranged the statements of the other one." Jean de Meun, *Le Roman de la Rose*, edited by E. Langlois (Paris: S.A.T.F., 1914-24), vv. 15216-24; Geoffrey Chaucer, *The Works of Geoffrey Chaucer*, edited by F. N. Robinson, 2nd ed. (Boston: Houghton, 1957), "General Prologue," vv. 725-46; Giovanni Boccaccio, *Decameron*, in *Opere di Giovanni Boccaccio*, pp. 27-28.

11. The process of self-authorization is evident in the prologue to the *Lais* of Marie de France at the moment she explains that she had first thought of translating ancient material from Latin to Romance. Others had already undertaken this activity, and so, she turns instead to writing down *lais* she has heard, *Les Lais de Marie de France*, edited by Jean Rychner (Paris: Champion, 1966), vv. 28-33.

12. Ed. Charles Livingston, Françoise R. Livingston, Robert H. Ivy, Jr. (Genève: Droz, 1972), p. 57.

13. Weimann, "Appropriation," p. 472.

14. Bonaventure Des Périers, *Nouvelles Récréations et Joyeux Devis*, edited by Krystyna Kasprzyk (Paris: Nizet, 1980), p. 5.

15. François Rabelais, *Oeuvres complètes*, 2 vols, edited by Pierre Jourda (Paris: Garnier Frères, 1967), 1: p. 5. English translations refer to *Gargantua & Pantagruel*, translated by J. M. Cohen (Harmondsworth, England: Penguin Books, 1983), p. 37.

16. Pierre-Yves Badel, "Rhétorique et Polémique dans les prologues de romans au Moyen Age." See also Tony Hunt (1970), pp. 2-3.

17. Approaching the issue of reader reception from a slightly different angle, Gérard Defaux argues that Rabelais is less interested in the legitimacy of allegorical interpretations than in how his own text will be received. In exploring the issue of allegorical interpretation and the "altior sensus" [loftier meaning], he hopes to win over his audience, "D'un problème l'autre: herméneutique de l' 'Altior Sensus' et 'Captatio lectoris' dans le prologue de Gargantua."

18. Cicéron, *Divisions de l'Art oratoire. Topiques*, translated by Henri Bornecque (Paris: Les Belles Lettres, 1960), VIII, 28. Cicero speaks of obtaining the goodwill, interest, and attention of his audience. In *L'Art poétique*, in *Oeuvres*, translated by

François Richard (Paris: Garnier Flammarion, 1967), 268, Horace states that poets strive to instruct and please and sometimes to instruct and please at the same time.

19. Weimann, "Appropriation," p. 470.

20. Minnis, p. 16. "Ancient rhetoricians had taught that everything which could form the subject of a dispute or discussion was covered by a series of questions, which, during successive generations of scholarship, was expanded into seven, namely, whom, which, why, in what manner, where, when, whence (or by what means). When applied to the grammatical discussion of a text, these *circumstanciae* provided the basis for a comprehensive and informative prologue"

21. Lionello Sozzi, *Les Contes de Bonaventure Des Périers*, p. 411. In "Notes on Des Périers' Nouvelles I, V, VII and XXII, and XLII," in *La Nouvelle française à la Renaissance*, edited by Lionello Sozzi (Geneva/Paris: Editions Slatkine, 1981), James W. Hassel, Jr. traces the sources of the maxim in France as far back as 1456, where it was used in the *Petit Jehan de Saintré* of Antoine de la Sale, p. 297. In tracing its use in France, Hassel cites as his last example Tabourot's *Les Bigarrures du seigneur Des Accords*, Quatriesme Livre (1585). I have found another use of the maxim in the prologue to Cholières's *Après-disnees*, published in 1587 in Paris by Jean Richter. The maxim suggests a positive attitude toward life. Cholières specifically opposes it to "ceux qui ont envie de farcir leur panse et epicuriser" [those who feel like stuffing their belly and living it up,] and so, as Sozzi indicates, the maxim is not to be interpreted in the hedonistic sense, *Les Après-disnees du seigneur de Cholieres* (Paris: Jean Richter, 1587), p. vii. When the early editions of sixteenth century works are cited in the present study, we have modernized the spelling only to the extent that a distinction is made between *i* and *y*, *u* and *v*. Abbreviations are spelled out.

22. In Badel's typology of Medieval prologues, type one always begins with a "sentence de portée générale", p. 84.

23. Marguerite de Navarre, *L'Heptaméron* (Paris: Garnier Frères, 1967), p. 9. For the English translation of most of the prologue, see Marcel Tetel, "Marguerite de Navarre: The *Heptameron*, a simulacrum of Love," in *Women Writers of the Renaissance and Reformation*, edited by Katharina M. Wilson (Athens, Ga.: University of Georgia Press, 1987), pp. 108–09.

24. Laurent Jenny, "La Stratégie de la forme," *Poétique* 27 (1976), p. 266.

25. In his "Le Prologue de *l'Heptaméron* et le processus de production de l'oeuvre," Philippe de Lajarte addresses the double strategy of inscribing history in fiction (through references to François I and madame Marguerite) and fiction in history (Parlamente's plan to present the finished work to members of the Court), in *La Nouvelle française à la renaissance*, pp. 397–423.

26. *Propos rustiques de Maistre Leon Ladulfi champenois*, à Lyon par Jean de Tournes, (1547), p. 10. Also in *Conteurs français du XVIme siècle*, edited by Pierre Jourda (Paris: Gallimard, 1956), p. 604. References will be made to the Jourda edition.

27. Hunt, "The Rhetorical Background," p. 1.

28. Michel Zink traces the emergence of literary subjectivity to the interventions and explanations by Medieval authors of romance concerning their efforts to make the ancient works and legends available to those who did not read Latin," *La Subjectivité littéraire*, p. 31.

29. Louise Labé, *Oeuvres complètes*, edited by Enzo Guidici (Genève: Droz, 1981), p. 17, 11. pp. 1–17. English translations of the *Débat de Folie et d'Amour* are taken from the article by Jeanne Prine, "Louise Labé, Poet of Lyon," in *Women Writers of*

NOTES TO CHAPTER 1

the Renaissance and Reformation, edited by Katharina Wilson (Athens, Ga.: University of Georgia Press, 1987), pp. 132–157.

30. Hélène Cixous, "Le Rire de la Méduse," *L'Arc* (1975), pp. 39–54.

31. "Il s'agit d'une intertextualité que le lecteur ne peut pas ne pas percevoir, parce que l'intertexte laisse dans le texte une trace indélibile, une constante formelle qui joue le rôle d'un impératif de lecture, et gouverne le déchiffrement du message dans ce qu'il a de littéraire, c'est-à-dire son décodage selon la double référence. Cette trace de l'intertexte prend toujours la forme d'une aberration à un ou plusieurs niveaux de l'acte de communication: elle peut être lexicale, syntaxique, sémantique, mais toujours elle est sentie comme la déformation d'une norme ou une incompatibilité par rapport au contexte. Donc une non-grammaticalité." [It is an intertextual reference which the reader cannot fail to notice, because the intertext leaves an indelible trace in the text, a formal constant that works as a reading imperative, and governs the decoding of the literary aspects of the message, namely its decoding in terms of a double reference. This trace of the intertext always takes the form of an aberration on one or several levels of the communicative act: it can be lexical, sytactical, semantic, but it is always experienced as a deformation of norm or an incompatibility in relationship to the context. Hence, an ungrammaticality, *La Pensée* 215 (1980): pp. 5–6., My thanks to François Rigolot for bringing this article to my attention. See also his article, "Gender vs. Sex Difference in Louise Labé's Grammar of Love," in *Rewriting the Renaissance: The Discourses of Sexual Difference in Early Modern Europe,* edited by Margaret W. Ferguson, Maureen Quilligan, and Nancy J. Vickers (Chicago: University of Chicago Press, 1986), pp. 287–298.

32. *Decameron,* edited by Cesare Segre, p. 8. Le Maçon translates the same passage as "Je veulx et entendz pour le secours de celles qui ayment (car il ne fault aux autres que lesguille, le fuzeau et le rouet)" [I wish and look to the help of those women who love (for the needle, spindle, and spinning wheel are enough for the others)] f. 2.

33. For a description of the hypogram as the word's descriptive system, see Riffaterre, *Semiotics of Poetry* (Bloomington: Indiana University Press, 1978), p. 43.

34. Weimann, "Appropriation," p. 472.

35. Michel de Montaigne, *Oeuvres complètes,* p. 9. All translations refer to *The Complete Essays of Montaigne,* translated by Donald M. Frame (Stanford, Calif.: Stanford University Press, 1976), p. 2. This passage implicitly alludes to Montaigne's idea of the consubstantial relationship between his life and his text. Only years later in an addition to the essay "Du démentir" will the author fully develop the idea: "Je n'ay pas plus faict mon livre que mon livre m'a faict, livre consubstantiel à son autheur, d'une occupation propre, membre de ma vie," [I have no more made my book than my book has made me—a book consubstantial with its author, concerned with my own self, an integral part of my life] (II, xviii, 648c; 504c).

36. On the publication of the third book of *Essais* in 1588, he seems to reappraise the extent of the author's property rights on his work: "Premierement, par ce que celuy qui a hypothecqué au monde son ouvrage, je trouve apparence qu'il n'y aye plus de droict" [First, because when a man has mortgaged his work to the world, it seems to me that he has no further right to it] (III, ix, 941b; 736b).

37. He is reported to have reiterated this concept when he presented his work to Henri III in 1580: "Sire, il faut donc nécessairement que je plaise à votre majesté, puisque mon livre lui est agréable, car il ne contient autre chose qu'un discours de ma vie et de mes actions," [Sire, I *must,* of necessity, please your majesty, since my book pleases you, because it contains nothing other than the narrative of my life and deeds,] cited by Thibaudet and Rat, xviii.

38. Barry Lydgate, "Mortgaging One's Work to the World: Publication and the Structure of Montaigne's *Essais*," *PMLA* 96, 2 (1981), p. 212.

39. See the insightful article by François Rigolot, "Référentialité, intertextualité, autotextualité dans les *Essais* de Montaigne," *Oeuvres et Critiques* VIII, 1-2 (1983), pp. 87-101.

40. Claude Blum explains that Montaigne's ambivalence towards classical authors is rooted in his need to show that the process of reflection on which the *Essais* is based begins with himself. It is not his readings which make him reflect but rather thought and self-reflection that lead him to the authors of the past, "Ecrire le 'moi': J'adjoute, mais je ne corrige pas," in *Montaigne* (1580–1980). Actes du colloque international (Paris: A.-G. Nizet, 1983), p. 45.

41. Hunt, p. 4.

Chapter 2. *Nue vérité ou invention poétique?*

1. *L'Heptaméron*, 9. Colette Winn has shown how Marguerite's insistence on truth in distinguishing her enterprise from that of Boccaccio is an essential element of the art of narrative seduction, "An Instance of Narrative Seduction: The *Heptaméron* of Marguerite de Navarre," *Symposium* 39, 3 (1985), pp. 217–226. In her recent book, *Fiction in the Archives: Pardon Tales and their Tellers in Sixteenth Century France*, Natalie Zemon Davis speaks of the use of historical details in pardon tales or letters of remission to give the "flavor of the actual" to the account (Stanford, Calif.: Stanford University Press, 1987), p. 29.

2. Roger Dubuis, *Les Cent Nouvelles Nouvelles et la tradition de la nouvelle en France au Moyen Age* (Grenoble: Presses Universitaires de Grenoble, 1973), p. 29.

3. William Nelson, *Fact or fiction: The Dilemma of the Renaissance Storyteller* (Cambridge, Mass.: Harvard University Press, 1973), p. 28.

4. L'Abbé Pierre Le Fèvre, dit Fabri, *Le Grant et Vrai Art de pleine rhétorique*, 3 vols., edited by Alexandre Héron (Paris: A. Lestringant, 1889–90), 1: p. 18. Cicéron, *Divisions de l'art oratoire. Topiques*, II: p. 5.

5. Jacques Amyot, *Les Vies des hommes illustres grecs et romains, comparées l'une avec l'autre par Plutarque de Chaernée translatée de grec en françois* (Paris: Michel Vascosan, 1559): "pource qu'ils ne monstrent pas seulement comme il faut faire, mais aussi impriment affection de le vouloir faire. . . . Aussi le fait elle [Histoire] avec plus de pois et plus de gravité, que ne font les inventions et compositions poëtiques, dautant qu'elle ne se sert iamais que de la nue verité et la poësie ordinairement enrichit les choses qu'elle loue, par dessus le merite. . . ." [because they not only show how one should go about it but also transmit a desire to do it. . . . So too, [history] does it with more weight and seriousness of purpose than do fabrications and poetic works, all the more since it only uses naked truth and since poetry usually embellishes the things it praises beyond their true merit] (iiii r°). Where abbreviations are used in the text, I have written the words in full as I will for all citations from Renaissance editions.

6. Dubuis, pp. 21–24. In *Narrative Imagination. Comic Tales by Philippe de Vigneulles* (Lexington, Kentucky: University Press of Kentucky, 1977), Armine Avakian Kotin assigns the following meanings to the word *nouvelle* in the context of Vigneulles' *Cent Nouvelles Nouvelles* (1515): event, an event recounted, an event broadcast to the general public, an event told aloud in a particular context or session, and finally, an event told in a particular setting and written down to read by others, p. 22.

7. Hayden White, *Tropics of Discourse. Essays in Cultural Criticism* (Baltimore:

NOTES TO CHAPTER 2

Johns Hopkins University Press, 1985), p. 122. Glyn P. Norton shows how the aesthetic criteria of consistency and verisimilitude mediate between "the pedestrian elements of historical truth and the high-flown fancies of poetic falsehood," "French Translations and the Dialectic of Myth and History," *Renaissance and Reformation/ Renaissance et Réforme* 5, 5 (1981): pp. 189–201.

8. Nelson, *Fact or Fiction*, pp. 30–31.

9. Nelson, *Fact or Fiction*, p. 59.

10. Nelson likens the author who parodies the historian to the person at a fancy dress ball who wants to be admired for his costume but not mistaken for the figure he is impersonating. "As Federico remarks in the Second Book of *Il Cortegiano*, a young man who masquerades as an old man should so clothe himself as to betray the nimbleness of his person," p. 67.

11. Philippe de Vigneulles, *Les Cent Nouvelles Nouvelles*, edited by Charles H. Livingston with Françoise R. Livingston and Robert H. Ivy, Jr. (Geneva: Droz, 1972), pp. 57–58.

12. Cicero, II, 5–V, p. 16. Fabri, 1: pp. 20–21.

13. In his address to the reader at the start of the *Grand Parangon des Nouvelles Nouvelles*, Nicolas de Troyes refers to himself as a "simple cellier," ed. Krystyna Kasprzyk (Paris: Didier, 1970), p. 5. Françoise Joukovsky notes the origin of the word as the Latin *cellarius*, clerk, *La Nouvelle Fabrique des excellents traicts de verité*, edited by Françoise Joukovsky (Paris: Droz, 1983), p. xxi.

14. Cicero comments that the appropriate style is neither too groomed or labored, Cicero VI, p. 19. In *The Motives of Eloquence* (New Haven: Yale University Press, 1976), Richard A. Lanham remarks, "The honest style is self-conscious, proclaims its designs on you," p. 22. Colette Winn mentions the seductive power of plain speech, "An Instance of Narrative Seduction," p. 219.

15. Gérard Genette, *Seuils*, p. 192.

16. Brunetto Latini's *Li Livres dou Tresor* refers to "li faiz" as a narrated incident. The "facteur" would thus correspond to the one who is narrating, in *Collection de documents inédits sur l'histoire de France*, 3: p. 519.

17. Vigneulles conforms to what Nelson calls the Renaissance turning away from the "wild dreams of the Medieval romancers" in favor of plausible contemporary events, p. 50. The narrator's insistence that these tales are to be transmitted orally or in writing underscores the vitality of the narrative tradition. For a study of the Renaissance reaction against the chivalric novel, see Marc Fumaroli, "Amyot and the Clerical Polemic against the Chivalric Novel," *Renaissance Quarterly* 38, 1 (1985): pp. 22–40.

18. Although decidedly more original than Nicolas de Troyes, Philippe de Vigneulles masks his borrowing. As Livingston has demonstrated, Tale 94 is a direct borrowing from the *Decameron*, but Vigneulles resituates it in Metz, and claims that if we have heard it before, it is only because the two husbands in question have broadcast it in a great many places ("en plusieurs lieux"), p. 372; Livingston, p. 38.

19. Bonaventure Des Périers, *Nouvelles Récréations et Joyeux Devis*, p. 12.

20. See the long note she devotes to attempts to date the peace in question, *Nouvelles Récréations*, p. 13.

21. In refusing to be upset by things over which he has no control, Des Périers approaches Rabelais's notion of *Pantagruélisme*, "gayeté d'esprit conficte en mespris des choses fortuites," "Prologue," *Quart Livre, Oeuvres complètes*, 2: p. 12; [lightness of spirit compounded of contempt for the chances of fate,] *Gargantua & Pantagruel*, p. 439.

22. Emile Benveniste remarks, "La langue doit par nécessité ordonner le temps à

partir d'un axe, et celui-ci est toujours et seulement du discours. . . . le seul temps inhérent à la langue est le présent axial du discours, et que ce présent est implicite" [Language must by necessity organize time along an axis, and this is always and only the axis of discourse. . . . the only time which is built into language is the axial present of discourse, and this present is implicit,] *Problèmes de linguistique générale* (Paris: Gallimard, 1974), pp. 74–75.

23. Jean Rychner calls the unexpected twist the "trait saillant," review of *Forerunners of the French Novel* by Janet M. Ferrier, *Bibliothéque d'Humanisme et Renaissance* 17 (1955): pp. 332–34.

24. Noël du Fail, *Propos rustiques*, in *Conteurs français du XVIe siècle*, p. 605. In "Le Dessein des *Propos rustiques*, G. A. Perouse links Du Fail's play with time and setting with the *facétie*. Pérouse argues that Du Fail had begun with the idea of poking fun at the nostalgic *propos* of his elders, and ends up admiring them, *Etudes des seiziémistes offerts à V. L. Saulnier* (Genève: Droz, 1980), pp. 137–68.

25. In *The Cornucopian Text* (Oxford: the Clarendon Press, 1979), Terence Cave studies the impact of Erasmus' discussion of *enargeia* on the poetical theory of the Renaissance, pp. 27–34.

26. Jacques Yver, *Le Printemps*, in *Les Vieux conteurs français*, edited by Paul Jacob (Paris: Société du Panthéon Littéraire, 1841), p. 521. All references will be made to this edition.

27. Nancy Regalado, *Poetic Patterns in Rutebeuf* (New Haven: Yale University Press, 1970), p. 262.

28. In his *Livres dou Tresor*, Latini advises: "tu doiz dire au commencement de ton prologue que tu conteras grans noveles ou grans choses, ou qui ne semblent pas creables, ou qui touchent à touz homes" [you must say at the outset of your prologue that you will recount great tales or great things, or things which do not seem believable, or things which concern all men,] 3: p. 519. The recent wars of religion have touched everyone, and Yver makes this point in the opening of his work. Rabelais's Prologue to the *Tiers Livre* makes a similar use of historical reference where he describes "un chascun aujourd'huy soy instantement exercer et travailler, part à la fortification de sa patrie et la defendre, part au repoulsement des ennemis, et les offendre," *Oeuvres complètes*, 1: p. 397; [everyone today busily and earnestly working, some at the fortification and defence of their country, some in repelling the enemy, some in attacking them,] *Gargantua & Pantagruel*, p. 283.

29. Philippe d'Alcripe, *La Nouvelle Fabrique des excellents traicts de verité* (Paris: Droz, 1983). Joukovsky dates the publication of the work from around the time of Philippe's death in 1581, p. xciv.

30. Béroalde de Verville, *Le Moyen de Parvenir*, Fac simile et transcription par Hélène Moreau et André Tournon, 2 vol. (Aix-en-Provence: Université de Provence, 1984), 1: p. 2. Ilana Zinger sees the opening as a recasting of a passage from an anonymous work, "La Permission aux servantes de coucher avec leurs maistres." See Zinger, *Structures narratives du Moyen de parvenir de Béroalde de Verville* (Paris: Nizet, 1979), p. 70. See also Michel Jeanneret, *Des mets et des mots. Banquets et Propos de table à la Renaissance* (Paris: José Corti, 1987), pp. 221–45.

31. The *indiction* goes back to Roman property taxes assessed every fifteen years, and the *lustre* or *lustrum* relates to a Roman rite of purification performed every five years after the census taking.

32. See Rabelais's portrait of Socrates in *Gargantua, Oeuvres complétes*, 1:6: "le visaige d'un fol, simple en meurs . . . tousjours riant, tousjours beuvant d'autant à un chascun, tousjours se guabelant, tousjours dissimulant son divin sçavoir"; [his idiotic face. . . . his manners were plain . . . he was always laughing, always drinking

glass for glass with everybody, always playing the fool, and always concealing his divine wisdom,] *Gargantua & Pantagruel,* p. 37.

33. Michel Foucault, *Les Mots et les choses* (Paris: Gallimard, 1966), p. 55; *The Order of Things* (New York: Vintage Books, 1971, p. 40.

34. In *Words and the Man in French Renaissance Literature* (Lexington, Ky.: French Forum, 1983), Barbara C. Bowen speaks of Béroalde's "flouting, not just most of our rules for a book, but the traditional rules for a banquet," p. 118. See also her article, "Béroalde de Verville and the Self-Destructing Book," in *Essays in Early French Literature presented to Barbara M. Craig,* edited by Norris J. Lacy and Jerry C. Nash (York, S.C.: French Literature Publications, 1982). pp. 163–77. Of Béroalde's "archi-banquet," we refer readers to Jeanneret's *Des mets et des mots,* pp. 221–45.

35. Richard L. Regosin, "The Boundaries of Interpretation: Self, Text, Contexts in Montaigne's *Essays,*" in *Renaissance Rereadings. Intertext and Context,* edited by Maryanne Cline Horowitz, Anne J. Cruz, and Wendy A. Furman (Urbana: University of Illinois Press, 1988), pp. 20–21. As Gisèle Mathieu-Castellani has demonstrated, Montaigne and his contemporary storytellers were less interested in the painstaking recording of events than in the depiction of the customs and habits that give a composite picture of human behavior, *Montaigne. L'Ecriture de l'essai* (Paris: Presses Universitaires de France, 1988), p. 73.

Chapter 3. Sampling the Book

1. *Les Mots et les choses,* p. 32; *The Order of Things,* p. 17: "Jusqu'à la fin du XVIe, la ressemblance a joué un rôle bâtisseur dans la savoir de la culture occidentale. C'est elle qui a conduit pour une grande part l'exégèse et l'interprétation des textes, c'est elle qui a organisé le jeu des symboles, permis la connaissance des choses visibles et invisibles, guidé l'art de les représenter." [Up to the end of the sixteenth century, resemblance played a constructive role in the knowledge of Western culture. It was resemblance that largely guided exegesis and the interpretation of texts; it was resemblance that organized the play of symbols, made possible knowledge of things visible and invisible, and controlled the art of representing them.]

2. Béroalde de Verville, *Moyen de Parvenir,* p. 27: "Ces sages et prudents prestres qui nomment leur breviaire leur femme."

3. *Les Mots et les choses,* pp. 34–35; *The Order of Things,* p. 19.

4. Hayden White, *Tropics of Discourse,* p. 91; *Les Mots et les choses,* p. 41; *The Order of Things,* p. 26.

5. *Tropics of Discourse,* p. 91.

6. Paul Ricoeur, *La Métaphore vive* (Paris: Editions du Seuil, 1975), p. 241. Discussing the work of Paul Henle, Ricoeur associates the effect of metaphor or the way we feel about a represented object with the poetic function of the metaphor.

7. In *Seuils,* Gérard Genette describes the themes of how as a critical function of the preface, p. 194. He explains that one can set up a good reading of the text by giving explicit directives, but also by providing the readers with the necessary information to allow them to carry on an informed reading of the text.

8. Ricoeur, p. 296. Ricoeur relies heavily on Nelson Goodman's work in *Languages of Art, an Approach to the Theory of Symbols* (Indianapolis, Ind.: The Bobbs-Merrill Co., 1968), pp. 69–73. Ricoeur here quotes Goodman.

9. Ricoeur makes a distinction between the rhetorical function of the metaphor—persuading through ornamentation (p. 31)—and its poetic function—developing the power to reorganize the way we view thinigs (p. 297).

10. As Raymond La Charité has pointed out, Alcibiades' portrait of Socrates, whom he compares to the Silenus box, gay and grotesque on the outside but full of precious drugs, competes with the more serious Erasmian context, in which Christ is the ultimate Silenus figure, "Lecteurs et lectures dans le prologue de *Gargantua*."

11. Both Raymond La Charité and Gérard Defaux underscore the link between writing and reading in the *Gargantua* prologue. La Charité, p. 268; Gérard Defaux, "D'un problème l'autre: herméneutique de l' 'altior sensus' et 'captatio lectoris' dans le prologue de *Gargantua*," p. 209.

12. In referring to the horizon of expectation, Hans Robert Jauss notes that for the reader, the new text evokes a set of expectations and rules which previous texts have established and with which the reader is familiar. Such rules can be respected or modified at will, *Pour une esthétique de la réception*, p. 51. Among the elements to be considered in reconstructing the reader's disposition towards a new text are: the norms or poetics of a certain genre, the implicit relationship linking the new text to notable texts considered in the historical context of the new work, and the opposition between fiction and reality—the poetic and the practical function of language. The opposition allows the readers to make comparisons not only with other works but between the world of the text before them and their own personal experience.

13. Ricoeur, p. 308. Northrop Frye, *Anatomy of Criticism* (Princeton: Princeton University Press, 1957), p. 80, pp. 302–14.

14. In *Collection de documents inédits sur l'histoire de France*, 3: p. 494.

15. In an interesting extension of the container/book metaphor, the Rabelaisian *tonneau*, as distinct from the barrel of Diogenes, is prized for its contents.

16. Several efforts to analyze the syntax of the Diogenes episode have revealed a degree of cynicism on the narrator's part concerning the validity of the frantic efforts of both the Corinthians and the French in preparing for war. François Rigolot, *Les Langages de Rabelais*, p. 100–101. Floyd Gray, *Rabelais et l'écriture*, p. 25.

17. As Barbara Bowen reminds us, the Renaissance writer and reader were steeped in a serious, moralizing tradition of *eruditio*, based on a respect for literary and social convention, *Words and the Man in French Renaissance Literature*, p. 25.

18. *Les Nouvelles Récréations et Joyeux Devis*, p. 16. Philippe de Vigneulles, *Les Cent Nouvelles Nouvelles*, pp. 57–58. Des Périers is not the first to use the mercantile metaphor in his prefatory remarks. The anonymous author of the *Cent Nouvelles Nouvelles*, written around 1460, speaks of the fabric, cut, and styling of his tales: "aussi pource que l'estoffe, taille et fasson d'icelles est d'assez fresche memoire et de myne beaucoup nouvelle" [also because the fabric, cut, and styling of these are of quite recent date and very new look,] *Conteurs français du XVIe siècle*, p. 19.

19. Le Seigneur de Cholières, *Les Après-disnees du Seigneur de Cholières* (Paris: Jean Richer, 1587), vii r°.

20. Guillaume Bouchet, *Les Serées de Guillaume Bouchet, Sieur de Brocourt*, edited by C. E. Roybet, 6 vol. (Paris: Alphonse Lemerre, 1873–82), I, p. iv. See Hope H. Glidden, *The Storyteller as Humanist: The Serées de Guillaume Bouchet* (Lexington, Ky.: French Forum, 1981) and Michel Jeanneret, *Des mets et des mots. Banquets et propos de table à la Renaissance*, pp. 175–180.

21. Gérard Genette, *Seuils*, p. 193.

22. Barbara C. Bowen comments on the contrast between the free, lively, and irreverent introduction to Béroalde de Verville's symposium and the straightforward, even reverent exposition of the rules for a banquet set forth by Bouchet, p. 168.

23. Jacques Yver, *Le Printemps*, in *Les Vieux Conteurs français*, p. 521.

24. In her letter to her cousin, Madame Minerve. Jeanne Flore follows a similar progression from oral tales to written tales to printed work. Her statement is straight-

forward, unembellished by metaphor, and makes no claim for the superiority of the printed word over the oral transmission of tales except in pointing out that one can reach a wider audience. Jeanne Flore, *Contes amoureux*, ed. G. A. Perouse et al. (Lyon: Presses Universitaires de Lyon, 1980), p. 97.

25. Michel de Montaigne, *Essais*, I, xxviii, 181a; p. 135.

26. François Rigolot has adeptly explored the purloining or prolonging of La Boétie's deathbed scene as recreated in Montaigne's letter to his father. The letter and the promise to his friend to give him a place, becomes a signifier that possesses Montaigne throughout his life and creative efforts. "Montaigne's Purloined Letter," *Yale French Studies* 64 *(1983):* pp. 145–166.

27. For a discussion of the *autotexte*, see Lucien Dällenbach, "Intertexte et autotexte," *Poétique* 27 (1976): pp. 282–296. Dällenbach defines the autotext as an internal reduplification or doubling of the story—in part or in its entirety—either on the discursive or fictional level of the text, p. 283.

28. See Elias L. Rivers, *Quixotic Scriptures. Essays in the Textuality of Hispanic Literature* (Bloomington: Indiana University Press, 1983), p. 109. I am indebted to Edward Friedman for his initiation into the prefatory world of *Don Quixote* during a seminar on Renaissance satire which we taught together. Miguel de Cervantes Saavedra, *Don Quixote de la Mancha*, translated by Walter Starkie (New York: New American Library, 1979), p. 41.

29. Ricoeur, p. 237, citing Le Guern, *Sémantique de la métaphore et de la métonymie* (Paris: Larousse, 1973), p. 58.

30. Ricoeur, p. 311.

31. Lydgate, "Mortgaging One's Work to the World," p. 221.

Chapter 4. The Functions of the Prologue

1. *Seuils*, pp. 182–218. Of the typology of prefaces set up by Genette, only the *préface originale*, written at the time of the publication of the first edition, concerns us here, and only the *préface auctoriale*, composed by the author of the main text. In passing, we may allude to subsequent versions of the preface, but our primary concern lies with the original, authorial preface.

2. Genette, Seuils, p. 183. Minnis, p. 16. See also the first chapter of the present study.

3. See Werner Söderhjelm, *La Nouvelle française au XVe siècle* (Paris: Honoré Champion, 1910), ix–x; Roger Dubuis, "La Genèse de la nouvelle en France au Moyen Age," *Cahiers de l'Association Internationale des Etudes Françaises* 18 (1966): pp. 9–19; Jean Rychner, Review of *Forerunners of the French Novel* by Janet M. Ferrier, *Bibliothèque d'Humanisme et Renaissance* 17 (1955): pp. 332–34. *Pointe* is Söderhjelm's term, *trait saillant* is used by Rychner to refer to the unexpected turn or twist, often based on word play, at the end of the tale.

4. *Les Cent Nouvelles Nouvelles*, in *Conteurs français du XVIe siècle*, p. 19.

5. Roger Dubuis, *Les Cent Nouvelles Nouvelles et la tradition de la nouvelle en France au Moyen Age*, p. 13. It should be pointed out that Genette dates the self-contained preface from Marot's edition of the *Roman de la Rose* (1526). While not entitlted preface or prologue, the dedicatory letter addressed to the Duke of Burgundy carries out several prefatory functions in introducing the reader to the *Cent Nouvelles Nouvelles*.

6. Philippe de Vigneulles, *Les Cent Nouvelles Nouvelles*, pp. 57–58.

7. *Nouvelles Récréations et Joyeux Devis*, pp. 16–18.

8. Le Seigneur de Cholières, *Les Après-disnees du Seigneur de Cholières*, p. vii.

9. *Les Cent Nouvelles Nouvelles*, p. 58: "se les adventures qui se font en divers lieux et que journellement adviennent venoient à la connoissance d'aucun bon facteur, ilz pourroient faire et composer ung livre aussi bon que ceulx qui ont esté faict devant" [If the adventures going on in different places and happening every day came to the attention of a good narrator, they could make up and form a book as good as those made before.]

10. *Oeuvres complètes*, I; p. 8: "car en icelle bien aultre goust trouverez et doctrine plus absconce, laquelle vous revelera de très haultz sacremens et mysteres horrificques, tant en ce que concerne nostre religion que aussi l'estat politicq et vie oeconomicque." *Gargantua & Pantagruel*, p. 38: [For here you will find an individual savour and abstruse teaching which will initiate you into certain very high sacraments and dread mysteries, concerning not only our religion, but also our public and private life.]

11. Marguerite de Navarre, *L'Heptaméron*, p. 7: "car si nous n'avons quelque occupation plaisante et vertueuse, nous sommes en dangier de demeurer malades." To this remark made by Parlamente, Longarine adds, "Mais, qui pis est, nous deviendrons fascheuses, qui est une maladie incurable" [for if we don't have any pleasurable and honest pastime, we are in danger of remaining sick . . . . But worse, we'll become irksome, which is an incurable illness.]

12. Jacques Yver, *Le Printemps*, in *Les Vieux Conteurs français*, p. 522.

13. Béroalde de Verville, *Le Moyen de Parvenir*, p. 22.

14. Gerald Prince, "Récit et texte dans le *Moyen de Parvenir*," *Neophilologus* 65, 1 (1981): pp. 1–5.

15. Genette, *Seuils*, p. 186.

16. Michel de Montaigne, *Essais*, 9; 2.

17. Bénigne Poissenot, *L'Esté*, ed. Gabriel-A. Pérouse et Michel Simonin avec la collaboration de Denis Baril (Genève: Droz, 1987), p. 55.

18. Noël du Fail, *Propos rustiques*, in *Conteurs du XVIe siècle*, p. 607.

19. Guillaume Bouchet, *Les Serées*, p. iii.

20. Genette, *Seuils*, p. 194

21. Edward Said, *Beginnings. Intention and Method* (Baltimore: The Johns Hopkins University Press, 1978), pp. 90–95.

22. Madame Jeanne Flore, *Contes Amoureux*, p. 97.

23. Prince, "Récit et texte," p. 3.

24. Nicolas de Troyes, *Le Grand Parangon des Nouvelles Nouvelles* (choix), edited by Krystyna Kasprzyk (Paris: Marcel Didier, 1970).

25. *Nouvelles Récréations*, p. 14: "Ne vous chagrinez point d'une chose irremediable" [Don't get upset over something for which there is no cure.] *Gargantua*, p. 9: "interpretez tous mes faictz et mes dictz en la perfectissime partie; [Interpret all my deeds and words, therefore, in the most perfect sense,] *Gargantua & Pantagruel*, p. 39; *Tiers Livre*, p. 401: "Je recongnois en eulx tous une forme specificque et propriété individuale, laquelle nos majeurs nommoient Pantagruelisme, moienant laquelle jamais en maulvaise partie ne prendront choses quelconques ilz congoistront sourdre de bon, franc et loyal couraige" [For in them I detect that specific trait and individual quality which our ancestors used to call Pantagruelism; which assures me that they will never take in bad part anything that they know to spring from a good, honest, and loyal heart,] *Gargantua & Pantagruel*, p. 286.

26. Jonathan Culler, *On Deconstruction. Theory and Criticism after Structutalism* (Ithaca: Cornell University Press, 1982), p. 78.

27. *Seuils*, p. 192.

NOTES TO CHAPTER 4

28. *Les Serées*, p. xiii: "Que si vous accusez de folie ceux qui ont mis en jeu ces plaisanteries et risees, et moy de les avoir racontees, je pourroy à bon droict autant dire de vous, qui vous amusez à lire" [For if you accuse of folly those who have contrived these pleasant and joyful conceits, as well me of having told them, I could with good reason say as much of you, who delight in reading them.]

29. Genette, *Seuils*, pp. 200–202.

30. William Nelson, *Fact or Fiction. The Dilemma of the Renaissance Storyteller*, p. 59.

31. *Pantagruel*, p. 218: "car il en a esté plus vendu par les imprimeurs en deux moys qu'il ne sera acheté de Bibles en neuf ans."

32. Nelson, p. 59: "But it was characteristic of the Renaissance attitude I am describing to depreciate the value of the narrative component of the work, to refer to that component with a tolerance sometimes bordering on contempt, as a concession to human weakness of no real worth save as lured the reader to partake of the solid nourishment he might otherwise reject."

33. Genette, *Seuils*, p. 208.

34. Gabriel A. Perouse argues that Renaissance collections of tales from the time of the *Heptaméron* until the end of the sixteenth century were characterized by an increasing level of tension between the narration and the commentary, between *récit* and *propos*. Narration was in a state of flux, developing in one direction toward the conversational style of the essay, and in the other, towards the more developed narration of the novel, "De Montaigne à Boccace et de Boccace à Montaigne. Contribution à l'étude de la naissance de l'essai," in *La Nouvelle française à la Renaissance*, edited by Lionello Sozzi (Geneva/Paris: Editions Slatkine, 1981), pp. 13–40.

35. Bouchet, p. xxiv: "Que si le tiltre des Serees ne me deffend, voire qu'il soit occasion de me calomnier encores plus, que voulez que j'y face, puis que Heraclides mesmes n'a peu eviter que le tiltre de son livre n'ayt esté moqué" [For if the title of Evening Gatherings does not protect me, but provides an opportunity to slander me even more, what do you want me to do, since even Heraclides could not avoid having the title of his book ridiculed.]

36. In *Words and the Man in French Renaissance Literature*, Barbara Bowen points out the irony of using mostly titles designating written texts of all kinds in a work devoted to the presumably spoken words of a symposium, p. 112.

37. Gerald Prince, "Récit et texte," pp. 3–4.

38. Antoine Compagnon, *La Seconde Main ou le travail de la citation* (Paris: Editions du Seuil, 1979), p. 328. He defines the *périgraphie* as the intermediate zone between what is outside of the text and the text. It corresponds to Genette's *paratexte*.

39. Genette, *Seuils*, p. 205: "La plus importante, peut-être, des fonctions de la préface originale consiste en une interprétation du texte par l'auteur, ou, si l'on préfère, en une déclaration d'intention" [The most important of the functions of the original preface consists of an interpretation of the text by the author, or, if you prefer, a declaration of intention.]

40. Hélisenne de Crenne, *Oeuvres* (Geneva: Slatkine, 1977), p. ii. This edition is a reprint of the Estienne Grouleau edition of 1560.

41. I disagree with Genette's statement that Rabelais has run out of steam in the prologue to the *Quart Livre*. It is more a question of changing prefatory strategy. Des Périers learned early on that combining exposition and narration in the prolgoue was good strategy and provided a sampling of the work to come. He uses this strategy in the *Nouvelles Récréations*, composed prior to 1544. Genette creates a useful term for this sort of preface, "la préface élusive," and credits Rabelais, not Des Périers, with its invention, *Seuils*, p. 218.

42. Jacques Derrida, *Dissemination*, translated by Barbara Johnson (Chicago: University of Chicago Press, 1981), pp. 44–45. See also the French original, *La Dissémination*, pp. 52–53: "En tant que préface du livre, elle est la parole du père assistant et admirant son écrit, répondant de son fils, s'essoufflant, à soutenir, à retenir, à idéaliser, à ré-intérioriser, à maîtriser sa semence." When Cholières describes his two works, *Les Matinees* and *Les Après-disnees* as his substitute godsons, we are very close to Derrida's notion of the preface as the "parole du père," *Après-disnees*, ii r°.

43. Genette cites the prologue of *Don Quixote* as the most notable example of preterition, a device in which the author promises not to write a prologue and then proceeds to do so. Cervantes leads us to believe that the prologue weighed so heavily on his mind that he nearly abandoned the whole writing project. The author's statement gives an idea of the indispensable role the prologue played in the publication process. Without the prologue, he worries that his work will be judged unworthy. Miguel de Cervantes Saavedra, *Don Quixote de la Mancha*, p. 42. *Seuils*, p. 217.

44. Derrida offers a view of the preface as neither more or less privileged than the main text it introduces. The preface and the main text coexist in a continuing process of interplay and cooperate to produce the play and the pleasure of the text. *Dissemination*, p. 54; *La Dissémination*, p. 62.

Chapter 5. Bridging the Gap

1. Elizabeth Eisenstein, *The Printing Press as an Agent of Change*, 2 vols. (London: Cambridge University Press, 1979), pp. 88–89.

2. Guido Almansi, *The Writer as Liar. Narrative Technique in the Decameron* (London: Routledge and Kegan Paul Ltd., 1975), p. 4.

3. Almansi, *The Writer as Liar*, p. 13.

4. Almansi, *The Writer as Liar*, p. 15.

5. Almansi, *The Writer as Liar*, p. 15.

6. Almansi, *The Writer as Liar*, p. 15.

7. In *The Age of Bluff. Paradox and Ambiguity in Rabelais and Montaigne* (Urbana: University of Illinois Press, 1972), Barbara Bowen comments on the "spurious sort of *vraisemblance*" involved in trying to create a parody of a parody, and in implying that *Gargantua* is similar in frame of reference to *Pantagruel*, p. 55.

8. Lucien Febvre et Henri-Jean Martin, *L'Apparition du livre* (Paris: Albin Michel, 1971), pp. 124–28.

9. "The *Essais*' Dedications," *Romanic Review* 73, 4 (1983): pp. 401–410. In Book III and in later editions of the essays, Montaigne realizes that his essays go far beyond the original goals he has set. He now has to adjust to writing to a larger audience and in such a way that the *Essais* do not merely recreate his image and passage but gloss it as well.

10. On the subject of Montaigne's belief that even those who are with us every day do not penetrate the depths of the individual character, see Claude Blum, "Ecrire le 'moi': J'adjoute, mais je ne corrige pas," in *Montaigne (1580–1980). Actes du colloque international* (Paris: A. J. Nizet, 1983), pp. 36–53.

11. See Chapter Three of this study.

12. The blurring of the distinction between his life and the written record, or between the person and the portrait, is evident in Montaigne's words to Henri III, when he presents the King with the first edition of the *Essais*: "Sire, il faut donc que je plaise à votre Majesté, puisque mon livre lui est agréable, car il ne contient autre chose qu'un discours de ma vie et de mes actions" [Sire, I must, of necessity, please

your majesty, since my book pleases you, because it contains nothing other than the story of my life and deeds] (*Essais*, xviii, cited by Thibaudet and Rat).

13. Almansi, *The Writer as Liar*, p. 13.

14. Perouse tells us that Du Fail observes and learns to appreciate his region of Brittany as he paints it for the reader, "Le Dessein des *Propos rustiques*, in *Etudes seiziémistes offertes à V. L. Saulnier* (Genève: Droz, 1980), pp. 137–150.

15. Jacques Yver, *Le Printemps*, in *Les Vieux Conteurs français*, pp. 522–23.

16. See Barbara C. Bowen, *Words and the Man*, p. 112.

17. Derrida, *La Dissemination*, p. 67. In refusing the conventional form of the preface, which, as Derrida states, parades as a kind of phony present but is really written after the fact, Béroalde lets his readers chart their own course, and only puts in false clues to further impede their progress. The clues are part of the ongoing game of writing which knows no preface or afterword, *La Dissémination*, p. 13. See also *Dissemination*, translated by Barbara Johnson (Chicago: University of Chicago Press, 1981) p. 59; p. 7.

18. Of the *Moyen de Parvenir*, Gerald Prince comments: "Le livre se dé-livre. Il défie la somme. Il est inconsommable" [The book frees /unmakes/ unbooks itself. It challenges the whole. It is inexhaustible.] "Récit et texte dans le *Moyen de Parvenir*, p. 4.

19. Prince calls this skepticism "l'aptitude pour le mystère et pour le doute," [a penchant for mystery and doubt,] p. 5.

20. *La Dissémination*, p. 64; *Dissemination*, p. 56; Or sous sa forme de bloc protocolaire, la préface est partout, elle est plus grande que le livre" [And yet, beneath the form of its protocolic block, the preface is everywhere, it is bigger than the book.] The preface is not, according to Derrida, a single surface, but a mass or block ["bloc"], endowed with a formal function which he calls a "bloc protocolaire," 25; p. 18.

Chapter 6. Women Addressing Women

1. Jeanne Flore, *Contes amoureux par Madame Jeanne Flore*, ed. Gabriel A. Perouse et al. (Lyon: Presses Universitaires de Lyon, 1980), p. 97; Louise Labé, *Oeuvres complètes*, edited by Enzo Guidici (Genève: Droz, 1981), p. 17. There are several editions of the works of Hélisenne de Crenne, *Les Oeuvres* (Paris: Estienne Grouleau, 1560), Reprint (Genève: Slatkine, 1977); *Les Angoysses douloureuses qui procedent d'amours, Première Partie*, edited by Paule Demats (Paris: Les Belles Lettres, 1968), *Les Angoysses douloureuses qui procèdent d'amours, Première Partie*, edited by Jérôme Vercruysse (Paris: Lettres Modernes, 1968), and finally, Harry Renell Secor, Jr., Hélisenne de Crenne, *Les Angoysses douloureuses qui procedent d'amours (1538). A Critical Editions Based on the Original Text with Introduction, Notes, and Glossary*, dissertation Yale University, 1957, p. 3. I cite from the Secor edition, since my comments extend beyond the first part. The *Contes amoureux* and the *Angoisses douloureuses* were published in 1537 and 1538 respectively. See the Pérouse edition of the *Contes amoureux* for an explanation of the date of publication, p. 22. The preface of a recent edition of the works of Louise Labé contains some insightful comments on the *Debat de Folie et d'Amour;* see Louise Labé, *Oeuvres complètes*, edited by François Rigolot (Paris: Flammarion, 1986). English translations of the works of Hélisenne de Crenne and Louise Labé come from *Women Writers of the Renaissance and Reformation*, edited by Katharina M. Wilson (Athens: University of Georgia Press. 1987): Jeanne Prine, "Louise Labé: Poet of Lyon," pp. 132–157; Kittye Delle

Robbins-Herring, "Helisenne de Crenne: Champion of Women's Rights," pp. 177–218. Other tranlations are mine unless specified to the contrary. I would like to express my thanks to Diane Wood of Texas Tech University for her suggestions to an earlier version of this chapter. My thanks also to Colette Winn of Washington University for her perceptive comments.

2. *Nouvelles Récréations*, p. 17.
3. *L'Heptaméron*, p. 10.
4. *Cent Nouvelles Nouvelles*, 58, l. p. 48.
5. Du Fail, *Propos rustiques*; Philippe d'Alcripe, *La Nouvelle Fabrique*, edited by Françoise Joukovsky (Genève: Droz, 1983); Cholières, *Les Après-disnees*, Monsieur de la Motte-Messamé, *Les Passetemps* (Paris: Jean le Blanc, 1595).
6. Monique Wittig, "The Mark of Gender," in the *Poetics of Gender*, edited by Nancy K. Miller (New York: Columbia University Press, 1986), pp. 63–73.
7. Wittig makes this point in her discussion of the subject pronoun *elles* as opposed to *ils*, p. 69.
8. The editor notes that the rhymes of the *dixains* are all feminine, p. 95. For a discussion of the possible identity of Jeanne Flore, and whether she existed in flesh and blood bearing the actual name Jeanne Flore or was a pseudonym invented by a group of men and women writing in Lyon, see the excellent introduction to the edition of the *Contes amoureux* by Pérouse and his team of editors, p. 42. They categorically oppose the identification of Jeanne Flore as Hélisenne de Crenne on the basis of major stylistic and ideological differences, pp. 43–44. In "Madame Jeanne Flore and the *Contes amoureux:* A Pseudonym and a Paradox," *Bibliothèque d'Humanisme et Renaissance* 51, 1 (1989): pp. 123–133, Régine Reynolds-Cornell suggests mixed authorship of the *Contes amoureux*, with active participation by Clémont Marot. The fact that the work presents itself as a woman's work, with all of the appropriate traits, suggests that the group—if indeed the work was jointly authored—had in mind a distinct set of characteristics of feminine discourse. What is important to our argument is that the liminary pages of the *Contes amoureux* are addressed to an exclusively feminine audience.
9. François Rigolot (en collaboration avec Kirk D. Read), "Discours liminaire et identité littéraire. Remarques sur la préface féminine au XVIe siècle," *Versants* 15 (1989): pp. 75–98. See also Rigolot's study, "Louise Labé et les Dames Lionnoises: les ambiguités de la censure," in *Le Signe et le texte. Etudes sur l'écriture au XVIe siècle en France*, edited by Lawrence D. Kritzman (Lexington, Ky.: French Forum, 1990): pp. 13–25.
10. See Guidici's notes on Clémence de Bourges in Labé's *Oeuvres complètes*, p. 94. I regret that Ann Rosalind Jones's fine book, *The Currency of Eros* (Bloomington: Indiana University Press, 1990), was published just as I was in the final process of preparing the present manuscript. Her remarks on Louise Labé's provocative approach to the gender question complement the issues discussed in this chapter.
11. In 1572, Jacques Yver closely takes up the Boccaccian model to dedicate his preface to the beautiful and virtuous young ladies of France, *Le Printemps d'Yver* (Anvers: Guillaume Silvias, 1572), f. 2. In addressing the ladies as "vertueuses, gracieuses, et bien apprises demoiselles" [virtuous, gracious, and well-taught young ladies] or as "gentilles demoiselles" [kind young ladies,] he shows his tie with the *Decameron*. Like Boccaccio, he writes to bring relief to the gentle ladies: "lors que le trop de loisir vous ennuyera," [When too much free time troubles you] f. 4. Again, it is the male from outside who brings the ladies relief in the form of entertainment.
12. Hélène Cixous, "Le rire de la méduse," p. 43.
13. *Les Cent Nouvelles nouvelles*, 58, ll. pp. 39–43: "Sy prie et supplye à tous ceulx

et celles qui les liront ou orront qu'ilz preignent le bien qu'ilz y verront et fuyent le mal qu'ilz y trouveront et qu'ilz me pardonnent les faultes qui y sont et les mettent à leurs corrections et amandement" [So I beg and beseech those men and women who will read them or hear them to take the good that they see in them and flee the bad that they find there, and may they pardon me the flaws which are there and submit them to their own corrections and modifications.]

14. Hélène Cixous notes that it is in writing for women that woman affirms woman in a role other than the one reserved for her—the role of silence, "Le rire de la méduse," p. 43.

15. In "Le Prologue de l'*Heptaméron* et la processus de la production de l'oeuvre," Philippe de Lajarte notes the opposition between the monologic, transcendental discourse of the primary narration and the dialogic discourse of the storytellers, where equality is the rule, p. 402.

16. See my article, "The Representation of Discourse in the Renaissance French *Nouvelle*: Bonaventure Des Périers and Marguerite de Navarre," *Poetics Today* 3 (1985): pp. 585–95.

17. Tale Twenty-two, the story of Sister Marie Héroët, is one such example.

18. Cathleen M. Bauschatz comments that Marie de Gournay assumes a male readership when she writes her Préface de 1595 for the reedition of Montaigne's *Essais*, "Marie de Gournay's 'Préface de 1595': A Critical Evaluation," *Bulletin de la Société des Amis de Montaigne* 34 (1986): pp. 73–82. It is curious that a woman reader who had discovered the pleasure of reading Montaigne at an early age should disregard women readers later on.

Afterword

1. Jacqueline T. Miller, *Poetic License. Authority and Authorship in Medieval and Renaissance Contexts* (New York: Oxford University Press, 1986), p. 3.

2. Eisenstein, *The Printing Press as an Agent of Change*, p. 122.

3. Lydgate, "Mortgaging One's Work to the World," p. 213.

4. *Des mets et des mots*, p. 249.

5. In *Des mets et des mots*, Jeanneret comments that in the French Renaissance and in the symposia, writing sought to escape itself by inscribing itself in the model of the spontaneous spoken word of sensory experience, p. 254.

6. Paul Zumthor, *La Lettre et la voix* (Paris: Editions du Seuil, 1987), p. 213.

7. Charles Perrault, *Contes*, édited by Jean-Pierre Collinet (Paris: Gallimard, Folio, 1981), pp. 49–53.

Selected Bibliography

Primary Sources

Alcripe, Philippe d'. *La Nouvelle Fabrique des excellents traicts de verité, livre pour inciter les resveurs tristes et melancholiques à vivre de plaisir.* Edited by Françoise Joukovsky. Paris: Droz, 1983.

Amyot, Jacques. *Les Vies des hommes illustres grecs et romains, comparées l'une avec l'autre par Plutarque de Chaernée translatée de grec en françois.* Paris: Michel Vascosan, 1559.

Benoît de Sainte-Maure. *Le Roman de Troie par Benoît de Sainte-Maure.* Edited by L. Constans. 6 vol. Paris: S.A.T.F., 1904–12.

Béroalde de Verville. *Le Moyen de Parvenir* (fac-similé). Edited by Hélène Moreau et André Tournon. 2 vols. Aix-en-Provence: Université de Provence, 1984.

———. *Le Moyen de Parvenir.* Edited by Paul L. Jacob. Paris: Bibliothèque Charpentier, 1903

Boccaccio, Giovanni. *Opere di Giovanni Boccaccio.* Edited by Cesare Segre. Milan: I. Mursia, 1978.

———. *Le Decameron de Messire Iehan Bocace Florentin, nouvellement traduict d'Italien . . .* Translated by Anthoine Le Maçon. Paris: Roffet, 1545.

———. *The Decameron.* Translated by Mark Musa and Peter Bondanella. New York/London: W.W. Norton, 1982.

Bouchet, Guillaume. *Les Serées de Guillaume Bouchet, Sieur de Brocourt.* Edited by C. E. Roybet. Paris: Alphonse Lemerre, 1873.

Les Cent Nouvelles Nouvelles. Conteurs français du XVIe siècle. Edited by Pierre Jourda. Bibliothèque de la Pléiade. Paris: Gallimard, 1956.

Cervantes Saavedra, Miguel de. *Don Quixote de la Mancha.* Translated by Walter Starkie. New York/Scarborough, Ontario: New American Library, 1979.

———. *Don Quixote de la Mancha.* Edited by Martin de Riquer. 2 vols. Barcelona: Editorial Juventud, 1958.

Chaucer, Geoffrey. *The Works of Geoffrey Chaucer.* Edited by F. N. Robinson. 2nd ed. Boston: Houghton, 1957.

Cholières, Le Seigneur de. *Les Après-disnees du Seigneur de Cholières.* Paris: Jean Richer, 1587.

Chrétien de Troyes. *Erec et Enide.* Edited by Mario Roques. Paris: Champion, 1963.

Cicéron. *Divisions de l'art oratoire. Topiques.* Translated by Henri Bornecque. Paris: Les Belles Lettres, 1960.

Dante Alighieri. *Tutte le opere.* Edited by Luigi Blasucci. Florence: G. C. Sansoni, 1965.

Des Périers, Bonaventure. *Nouvelles Récréations et Joyeux Devis I XC.* Edited by Krystyna Kasprzyk. Paris: Nizet, 1980.

Du Fail, Noël. *Propos rustiques de Maistre Leon Ladulfi champenois*. Lyon: Jean de Tournes, 1547.

———. *Propos rustiques de Maistre Leon Ladulfi. Conteurs français du XVIe siècle*. Edited by Pierre Jourda. Paris: Gallimard, 1956. 596–659.

Flore, Madame Jeanne. *Contes Amoureux par Madame Jeanne Flore*. Edited by Gabriel-A. Perouse et al. Lyon: Presses Universitaires de Lyon, 1980.

Héliesenne de Crenne. *Les Oeuvres*. Paris: Estienne Grouleau, 1560. Reprint. Genève: Slatkine, 1977.

———. *Les Angoysses douloureuses qui procedent d'amours* (Première partie). Edited by Paule Demats. Paris: Les Belles Lettres, 1968.

———. *Les Angoysses douloureuses qui procedent d'amours (1538). A Critical Edition Based on the Original Text with Introduction, Notes, and Glossary*. Edited by Harry Renell Secor, Jr. Dissertation Yale University, 1957.

———. *Les Angoysses douloureuses qui procèdent d'amours (Première Partie)*. Edited by Jérôme Vercruysse. Paris: Les Belles Lettres, 1968.

Jean de Meun. Le Roman de la Rose. Edited by E. Langlois. Paris: S.A.T.F., 1914–24.

Labé, Louise. *Oeuvres complètes*. Edited by Enzo Guidici. Genève: Droz, 1981.

Latini, Brunetto. *Li Livres dou Tresor. Collection de documents inédits sur l'histoire de France*. Edited by P. Chabaille. Paris: Imprimerie Impériale, 1863.

Le Fèvre, l'Abbé, dit Fabri. *Le Grant et Vrai Art de pleine rhétorique*. Edited by Alexandre Héron. 3 vol. Paris: A Lestringant, 1889–90.

Marie de France. *Les Lais de Marie de France*. Edited by Jean Rychner. Paris: Champion, 1966.

Marguerite de Navarre. *L'Heptaméron*. Edited by Michel François. Paris: Garnier Frères, 1967.

Montaigne, Michel de. *Oeuvres complètes*. Edited by Albert Thibaudet et Maurice Rat. Bibliothèque de la Pléiade. Paris: Gallimard, 1962.

———. *The Complete Essays*. Translated by Donald M. Frame. Stanford, Calif.: Stanford University Press, 1976.

Nicolas de Troyes. *Le Grand Parangon des Nouvelles Nouvelles*. Edited by Krystyna Kasprzyk. Paris: Didier, 1970.

Perrault, Charles. *Contes*. Edited by Jean-Pierre Collinet. Folio. Paris: Gallimard, 1981.

Poissenot, Bénigne. *L'Esté*. Edited by Gabriel-A. Perouse et Michel Simonin avec la collaboration de Denis Baril. Genève: Droz, 1987.

Rabelais, François. *Oeuvres complètes*. Edited by Pierre Jourda. 2 vols. Paris: Garnier Frères, 1962.

———. *Gargantua & Pantagruel*. Translated by J. M. Cohen. Harmondsworth, England/New York, N.Y.: Penguin Books, 1983.

Tabourot, Estienne. *Les Bigarrures du Seigneur des Accords*. Fac-similé de l'édition de 1588. Edited by Francis Goyet. 2 vols. Genève: Droz, 1986.

Vigneulles, Philippe de. *Les Cent Nouvelles Nouvelles*. Edited by Charles H. Livingston avec le concours de Françoise R. Livingston et Robert H. Ivy, Jr. Genève: Droz, 1972.

Yver, Jacques. *Le Printemps. Les Vieux Conteurs français*. Edited by Paul L. Jacob. Paris: Société du Panthéon Littéraire, 1841.

———. *La Printemps. Conteurs du XVIe siècle.* Bibliothèque de la Pléaide. Paris: Gallimard, 1956.

Secondary Sources

Austin, J. L. *How to do Things with Words.* Edited by J. O. Urmson. London: Oxford University Press, 1962.

Almansi, Guido. *The Writer as Liar. Narrative Technique in the Decameron.* London: Routledge and Kegan Paul Ltd., 1975.

Badel, Pierre Yves. "Rhétorique et Polémique dans les prologues de romans au Moyen Age," *Littérature* 20 (1975): pp. 81–83.

Bauschatz, Cathleen, M. "Marie de Gournay's 'Préface de 1595': A Critical Evaluation." *Bulletin de la Société des Amis de Montaigne* 34 (1986): pp. 73–82.

Benveniste, Emile. *Problèmes de linguistique générale.* Paris: Gallimard, 1974.

Blum, Claude, "Ecrire le 'moi' : J'adjoute, mais je ne corrige pas." In *Montaigne (1580–1980).* Actes du colloque international, pp. 36–53. Paris: A. G. Nizet, 1983.

Bowen, Barbara C. "Béroalde Verville and the Self-Destructing Book." In *Essays in Early French Literature presented to Barbara M. Craig.* Edited Norris J. Lacy and Jerry C. Nash, pp. 163–78. York, S.C.: French Literature Publications, 1982.

———. *Words and the Man in French Renaissance Literature.* Lexington, Ky.: French Forum, 1983.

Brush, Craig B. "Montaigne's Preface." *Teaching Language through Literature* 24, 2 (1985): pp. 27–36.

Cave, Terence. *The Cornucopian Text.* Oxford: The Clarendon Press, 1979.

Cixous, Hélène. "Le rire de la méduse." *L'Arc* 61 (1975): pp. 39–54.

Coleman, Dorothy. "The Prologues of Rabelais." *Modern Language Review* 62, 3 (1967): pp. 407–19.

Compagnon, Antoine. *La Seconde Main ou le travail de la citation.* Paris: Editions du Seuil, 1979.

Conley, Tom. "Un petit fait d'Yver." In *Textes et Intertextes. Etudes sur le XVIe siècle pour Alfred Glauser.* Edited by Floyd Gray et Marcel Tetel, pp. 49–67. Paris: A. G. Nizet, 1979.

Cortelazzo, Manlio e Paolo Zolli. *Dizionario etimologico della lingua italiana.* Vol. 4. Bologna: Zanichelli, 1985.

Culler, Jonathan. *On Deconstruction. Theory and Criticism after Structuralism.* Ithaca: Cornell University Press, 1982.

Dällenbach, Lucien. "Intertexte et autotexte." *Poétique* 27 (1976): pp. 282–96.

Davis, Natalie Zemon. *Fiction in the Archives. Pardon Tales and their Tellers in Sixteenth Century France.* Stanford Calif.: Stanford University Press, 1987.

Defaux, Gérard. "D'un problème l'autre : herméneutique de l'*altior sensus*' et '*captatio lectoris*' dans le prologue de *Gargantua*." *Revue d'Histoire Littéraire de France* 2 (1985): pp. 196–216.

Delle Robbins-Herring, Kittye. "Hélisenne de Crenne: Champion of Women's Rights." In *Women Writers of the Renaissance and Reformation.* Edited by Katharina M. Wilson, pp. 177–218. Athens, Ga./London: University of Georgia Press, 1987.

Derrida, Jacques. *La Dissémination.* Paris: Edition du Seuil, 1972.

———. *Dissemination*. Translated by Barbara Johnson. Chicago: The University of Chicago Press, 1972.

Dubuis, Roger. *Les Cent Nouvelles Nouvelles et la tradition de la nouvelle en France au Moyen Age*. Grenoble: Presses Universitaires de Grenoble, 1973.

———. "La Genèse de la nouvelle en France au Moyen Age." *Cahiers de l'Association Internationale des Etudes Françaises* 18 (1966): pp. 9–19.

Ducrot, Oswald et Tzvetan Todorov. *Dictionaire encyclopédique des sciences du langage*. Paris: Editions du Seuil, 1972.

Eisenstein, Elizabeth L. *The Printing Press as an Agent of Change*. Vol. 1. Cambridge University, 1979. 2 vols.

Febvre, Lucien et Henri-Jean Martin. *L'Apparition du livre*. Paris: Albin Michel, 1971.

Foucault, Michel. *Les Mots et les choses*. Paris: Gallimard, 1966.

———. *The Order of Things*. New York: Vintage Books/Random House, 1973.

Friedrich, Hugo. *Montaigne*. Translated by R. Rovini. Paris: Gallimard, 1970.

Frye, Northrop. *Anatomy of Criticism*. Princeton: Princeton University Press, 1957.

Fumaroli, Marc. "Amyot and the Clerical Polemic against the Chivalric Novel." *Renaissance Quarterly* 38, 1 (1985): pp. 22–40.

Genette, Gérard. *Seuils*. Paris: Editions du Seuil, 1987.

Glidden, Hope. "Recouping the text: The Theory and the Practice of Reading." *L'Esprit Créateur* 21, 2 (1981): pp. 25–37.

———. *The Storyteller as Humanist. The Serées of Guillaume Bouchet*. Lexington, Ky.: French Forum, 1981.

Gray, Floyd. *Rabelais et l'écriture*. Paris: A. G. Nizet, 1974.

Hassel, James W., Jr. "Notes on Des Périers' Nouvelles I, V, VII and XXII, and XLII." In *La Nouvelle française à la Renaissance*. Edited by Lionello Sozzi, pp. 297–306. Genève/Paris: Editions Slatkine, 1981.

Hunt, Tony. "The Rhetorical Background to the Arthurian Prologue: Tradition and the Old French Vernacular Prologues." *Forum for Modern Language Studies* 6, 1 (1972): pp. 320–44.

Jauss, Hans Robert. *Pour une esthétique de la réception*. Paris: Gallimard, 1978.

Jeanneret, Michel. *Des mets et des mots. Banquets et Propos de table à la Renaissance*. Paris: José Corti, 1987.

Jenny, Laurent. "La Stratégie de la forme." *Poétique* 27 (1976): pp. 257–81

Jones, Ann Rosalind. *The Currency of Eros. Women's Love Lyric in Europe, 1540–1620*. Bloomington: Indiana University Press, 1990.

Jordon, Constance. *Renaisance Feminism. Literary Texts and Political Models*. Ithaca: Cornell University Press, 1990.

Kotin, Armine Avakian. *Narrative Imagination. Comic Tales by Philippe de Vigneulles*. Lexington, Ky.: University Press of Kentucky, 1977.

La Charité, Raymond. "Lecteurs et lectures dans le prologue de *Gargantua*." *French Forum* 10 (1985): 261–70.

Lajarte, Philippe de. "Le Prologue de l'*Heptaméron* et le processus de production de l'oeuvre." in *La Nouvelle Française à la Renaissance*. Edited by Lionello Sozzi, pp. 397–424. Genève/Paris: Slatkine, 1981.

Lanham, Richard A. *The Motives of Eloquence*. New Haven: Yale University Press, 1976.

Larkin, Neil M. "The *Essais'* Dedications." *Romanic Review* 73, 4 (1983): pp. 401–410.

Lejeune, Philippe. *Le Pacte autobiographique.* Paris: Editions du Seuil, 1975.

Losse, Deborah N. *Rhetoric at Play. Rabelais and Satirical Eulogy.* Bern: Peter Lang, 1980.

———. "The Representation of Discourse in the Renaissance *Nouvelle.*" *Poetics Today* 5, 3 (1984), pp. 585–595.

Lydgate, Barry. "Mortgaging One's Book to the World: Publication and Structure of Montaigne's *Essais.*" *PMLA* 96, 2 (1981): pp. 210–223.

Mathieu-Castellani, Gisèle. *Montaigne. L'écriture de l'essai.* Paris: Presses Universitaires de France, 1988.

Miller, Jacqueline T. *Poetic Licence. Authority and Authorship in Medieval and Renaissance Contexts.* New York/Oxford: Oxford University Press, 1986.

Miller, Nancy K. *The Poetics of Gender.* New York: Columbia University Press, 1986.

Minnis, A. J. *Medieval Theory of Authorship. Scholastic Literary Attitudes in the Later Middle Ages.* London: Scolar Press, 1984.

Nelson, William. *Fact or Fiction. The Dilemma of the Renaissance Storyteller.* Cambridge, Mass.: Harvard University Press, 1973.

Norton, Glyn P. "French Renaissance Translations and the Dialectic of Myth and History." *Renaissance and Reformation/Renaissance et Réforme* 5, 5 (1981): pp. 189–201.

Ollier, Marie-Louise. "The Author in the Text: The Prologues of Chrétien de Troyes." *Yale French Studies* 51 (1974): pp. 26–41.

Pérouse, Gabriel-A. "Le Dessein des *Propos rustiques.*" In *Etudes Seiziémistes offertes à Monsieur le Professeur V. L. Saulnier.* pp. 137–50. Genève: Froz, (1980).

The Préface (Ouvertures, Prolégomènes, Préludes, Avis, Avant-Propos). Special Issue of *L'Esprit Créateur* 27, 3 (1987).

Prince, Gerald. "Récit et texte dans le *Moyen de parvenir.*" *Neophilologus* 65, 1 (1981): pp. 1–5.

Prine, Jeanne. "Louise Labé: Poet of Lyon." In *Women Writers of the Renaissance and Reformation,* pp. 132–57.

Prologues au XVIe siècle. Special Issue of *Versants* 15 (Nouvelle série) (1989).

Regalado, Nancy. *Poetic Patterns in Rutebeuf.* New Haven: Yale University Press, 1970.

Regosin, Richard L. "The Boundaries of Interpretation: Self, Text, Contexts." In *Renaissance Rereadings. Intertext and Context.* Edited by Maryanne Cline Horowitz, Anne J. Cruz, and Wendy A. Furman, pp. 18–32. Urbana: University of Illinois Press, 1988.

Reynolds-Cornell, Régine. "Madame Jeanne Flore and the *Contes amoureux:* A Pseudonym and a Paradox." *Bibliothèque d'Humanisme et Renaissance* 51, 1 (1989): pp. 123–133.

Ricoeur, Paul. *La Métaphore vive.* Paris: Editions du Seuil, 1975.

Riffaterre, Michael. "La Trace de l'intertexte." *La Pensée* 215: pp. 4–24.

———. *Semiotics of Poetry.* Bloomington/London: Indiana University Press, 1978.

Rigolot, François (en collaboration avec Kirk D. Read), "Discours liminaire et identité littéraire." *Versants* 15 (1989): pp. 75–98.

———. "L'Imaginaire du discours préfaciel: l'exemple de la Franciade. *Studi di letteratura francese* 12 (1986): pp. 231–248.

———. *Les Langages de Rabelais*. Etudes Rabelaisiennes X. Genève: Droz, 1972.

———. "Louise Labé et les Dames Lionnoises : les ambiguités de la censure." In *Le Signe et le texte. Etudes sur l'écriture au XVIe siècle en France*. Edited by Lawrence D. Kritzman, pp. 13–25. Lexington, Ky.: French Forum, 1990.

———. "Montaigne's Purloined Letter." *Yale French Studies* 64 1983, pp. 146–66.

———. Prolégomènes à une étude du statut de l'appareil liminaire des textes littéraires, *L'Esprit Créateur* 27, 3 (1987): pp. 7–18.

———. *Le Texte de la Renaissance*. Genève: Droz, 1982.

Rivers, Elias L. *Quixotic Scriptures. Essays in the Textuality of Hispanic Literature*. Bloomington: Indiana University Press, 1983.

Rychner, Jean. Rev. of *Forerunners of the French Novel*, by Janet M. Ferrier. *Bibliothèque d'Humanisme et Renaissance* 17 (1955): pp. 332–34.

Said, Edward. *Beginnings. Intention and Method*. Baltimore: The Johns Hopkins University Press, 1978.

Schultz, James A. "Classical Rhetoric, Medieval Prologues, and the Medieval Vernacular Prologue." *Speculum* 59 (1984): pp. 1–15.

Smith, Paul. "Le Prologue du *Pantagruel* : Une Lecture." *Neophilologus* 68 (1984): pp. 161–169.

Söderhjelm, Werner. *La Nouvelle française au XVe siècle*. Paris: Honoré Champion, 1910.

Sozzi, Lionello. *Les Contes de Bonventure Des Périers*. Torino: Giapichelli, 1965.

Starobinski, Jean. *Montaigne en mouvement*. Paris: Gallimard, 1982.

Tetel, Marcel. "Marguerite de Navarre: *The Heptameron*, a Similacrum of Love." In *Women Writers of the Renaissance and Reformation*, pp. 132–57.

Weimann, Robert. "Appropriation and Modern History in Renaissance Prose Narrative," *New Literary History* 14, 3 (1983): pp. 459–95.

White, Hayden. *Tropics of Discourse. Essays in Cultural Criticism*. Baltimore/London: Johns Hopkins University Press, 1985.

Wilson, Katharina M. *Women Writers of the Renaissance and Reformation*. Athens, Ga.: University of Georgia Press, 1987.

Winn, Colette H. "An Instance of Narrative Seduction: The *Heptaméron* of Marguerite de Navarre." *Symposium* 39, 3 (1985): pp. 217–26.

Zinger, Ilana. *Structures narratives du Moyen de Parvenir de Béroalde de Verville*. Paris: Nizet, 1979.

Zink, Michel. *La Subjectivité littéraire*. Paris: Presses Universitaires de France, 1985.

Zumthor, Paul. *La Lettre et la voix*. Paris: Editions du Seuil, 1987.

Index

Adam, 98
Aesop, 24, 84
Alcibiades, 23, 47–48, 114 n.10
Alcofrybas, 47, 59
Alexander, 43, 97
Allegorical interpretation, 23; Medieval practice, 23; names, 95; rejection, 38
Allegory, 40, 88, 107 n.17. *See also* Yver, Jacques
Almansi, Guido, 81, 87
Alphonse, King of Aragon, 70
Altior sensus, 107 n.17
Amyot, Jacques: *aux lecteurs*, 18; history, 34–35; history and life, 17; translator of Plutarch, 17; *Vie des hommes illustres*, 17. *See also* History
Anticipation, 103
Anticipatory function, 80
Antiquity, 95
Antonomasia, 58, 85
Appropriation, 21–22, 57, 106–7 n.6; definition, 20; honor, 30; muted sector, 28; property rights, 25; property status, 31; self, 29, 31, 48; self-characterization, 49; women's voice, 29. *See also* Labé, Louis
Argument a contrario, 60
Aristotle: distinction between prologue and proem, 15; laughter, 76
Artistic intent, 45
Artistic rules, 80, 81
Auctor, auctores, 21, 23, 24, 26, 27, 58, 107 n.10; Boccaccio, 30–31; definition, 20; exclusion, 32; male, 97
Auctoritas, 23, 32; definition, 20
Audience, 94; confined circle of women, 94, 99, 100; detractors, 42; expectations, 17; family, 31, 87; friends, 17, 27, 87; good man, 87; lack of consensus, 105 n.12; neighbors, 87; rural or rustic, 39; world, 87

Austin, J. L., 105 n.9
Author: as compiler, 20, 21, 36, 39, 62, 107 n.10; as translator, 20
Authority, 21, 23, 88; self, 31; source, 101
Authorization, 21, 22, 27, 57; definition, 20; Medieval, 15; self-inscription, 27, 36
Authorship, 101
Autotext: definition, 54, 115 n.27
Axial present of discourse, 112 n.22

Babel, 46
Badel, Pierre-Yves, 11, 23
Banquet: *propos de table*, 101
Bel-Accueil, le seigneur de, 88
Bene vivere et laetari [laetari et bene vivere], 75, 76
Benveniste, Emile, 112 n.22
Béroalde de Verville, 14; *Moyen de parvenir*, 42, 45–46, 59–60, 62, 63, 65, 71, 80, 89, 113 n.34, 119 n.17
Beuveurs/verolez, 82, 90
Blame: detractors, 71, 82, 83, 84, 85
Blum, Claude, 87, 110 n.40, 118 n.10
Blurred distinctions, 85
Boccaccio, Giovanni, 19, 21, 35, 73, 88, 96, 100; *la brigata*, 80; champion of the weaker sex, 94–95; *cornice*, 80; *Decameron*, 16, 17, 26–27, 40, 61, 63, 99, 120 n.11
Bodin, Jean, 43
Boethius, 19
Book [livre]: conventional look, 89; formal appearance, 11; Medieval concept, 20, 32; subversive look, 89; title page, 12
Book market: Lyon, Strassburg, Frankfurt, London, Madrid, 22
Book production: expanding markets, 63
Bouchet, Guillaume, 14, 17; dedicatory

epistle, 62; *Les Serées,* 51–52, 66–67, 69, 70–71, 76, 90
Bourges, Clémence de, 28, 90, 94, 118 n.7, 120 n.10
Bowen, Barbara C., 42, 113 n.34, 114 n.17, 114 n.22, 117 n.36
Burgundy, duke of: dedicatory epistle, 115 n.5

Cangrande della Scala: letter from Dante, 15
Captatio benevolentiae, 39, 41, 57; Dante, 16
Censorship by the Church, 64
Cents Nouvelles Nouvelles, Les (anonymous), 13, 33, 58, 64, 81, 87; Duke of Burgundy, 35
Cervantes, 118 n.43; *Don Quixote de la Mancha,* 54, 77, 115 n.28
Charles V, 37, 49
Charles VII, 36
Chaucer, Geoffrey, 21
Chinon, 84
Chivalric novel, 111 n.17
Cholières, le seigneur de, 13, 51, 59, 63, 76–77, 91, 102–3, 108 n.21, 118 n.42; *Aux liseurs,* 17; *Les Après-disnees,* 54–56, 58–61, 69–70, 73, 75; *Les Matinees,* 55
Chrétien de Troyes: *Erec et Enide,* 21
Chroniclers [chroniqueurs], 39, 40
Chronicles, 82; preface, 85
Cicero, 69, 107–8 n.18, 111 n.14; *De inventione,* 13, 16, 19; exordium, 24; prefatory goals, 15
Cincinnatus, 27
Circumstanciae, 57, 108 n.20
Cixous, Hélène, 29; transgression, 96
Claims: benefits, 59; book of all books, 60, 63; good faith, 62; historic, 59; identity, 32; moral, 59; paternity, 32; religious, 59; remedy, 59
Classical rhetoric, 19; *dispositio,* 36; *elocutio,* 36; subordinate *inventio,* 36; teaching, 19
Closure, 63
Commentary, 103
Communication: between author and reader, 18
Community of writers: women, 93
Compagnon, Antoine, 73

Consistency, 111 n.7
Consubstantiality, 109 n.35
Conte: definition, 13, 106 n.6; genre, 35; new look, 13; recent, 13. *See also* Nouvelle
Contemporary issues: grounding in, 102
Conter, 17
Conteurs, 68, 102; early, 81; prefatory strategies, 14; pre-publication jitters, 96; Renaissance, 13, 34, 58, 62, 71, 73, 90, 91; titles, 17
Conteuses, 94, 100, 102
Context: immediate, 55; foreign, 55
Corinthians, 48–49, 114 n.16. *See also* Rabelais, François,
Cornutus, 23
Couillatris, 84, 102
Criticism of men, 98, 101
Crotesque, 53

Da Buti, F., 15
D'Alcripe, Philippe (Philippe Le Picard), 91; *La Nouvelle Fabrique,* 41
Dällenbach, Lucien, 115 n.27
Dante: *Convivio,* 15; *Epistotle,* 15, 16; *Paradiso,* 15
Dauphin/Dauphine, 91, 100; distaste for rhetorical embellishment, 33
Davis, Natalie Zemon, 110 n.1
Dedicatory epistle, 73, 90, 91
Defaux, Gérard, 23, 47, 107 n.17, 114 n.11
Deictics, 105 n.9
Derrida, Jacques, 104 n.4, 118 n.42, 118 n.44
Des Périers, Bonaventure, 13, 18, 28, 32, 49, 50, 59, 76, 85–86, 90–91, 101, 111 n.21, 117 n.41; *Nouvelles Récréations et Joyeux Devis,* 12, 22, 24–26, 31, 37–38, 58, 63, 68, 64–65, 69, 75, 81; Plaisantin, 25; *préambule,* 17, 85
Detractors, 102
Devisants, 61, 41, 85, 88
Dialectic, 69
Diogenes, 23, 24, 49–50; *Le Tiers Livre,* 48; *tonneau,* 114 n.15. *See also* Rabelais, François
Dipsodie, 83
Direct speech, 50
Discours d'escorte, 79, 83, 101
Discours de femme, 100

INDEX

Discourse: spoken, 52; written, 52
Dissemination, 62
Distancing, 22
Donatus, 19
Ducrot, Oswald, 105 n.9
Du Fail, Noël, 13, 53, 61, 91, 112 n.24; *au lecteur*, 101; Leon Ladulfi, 27–28; *Propos rustiques*, 17, 27–28, 31, 80, 88; rusticity, 69
Duplicity: pact between narrator and reader, 35

Eisenstein, Elizabeth, 79, 101
Empowerment, 93
Emulation [*aemulatio*]: definition, 46. *See also* Likeness
Enargeia: definition, 39
Encouragement to publish, 93–94
Equality: gender, 99; grammar, 92, 99
Epitexte, 104 n.1
Erasmus: intertext, 47
Erudition [*eruditio*], 114 n.17
L'Esprit Créateur, 11
Essay: genre, 14
Estoire, 34, 106 n.6; definition, 20
Estranging device [*oestranenye*], 80, 81
Euripedes, 106 n.23
Exclusion: gender, 92; grammar, 92
Exemplaire de Bordeaux, 54
Exordium, 12, 57
Expectation: reader, 96
Eye witness, 61, 68

Fable: *mythos*, 48
Fabri, Pierre, 34
Facétie, 77, 112 n.24
Fari: speech, 18
Febvre, Lucien, 12
Feminine community, 99
Fiction: inscribed in history, 108 n.25; plausible, 45
Fictional contract, 63
Fiction and history: different standards, 42
Flaubert, Gustave, 12
Flavor of the actual, 110 n.1
Fleur d'Amour, Ferme-Foy, les seigneurs de, 88
Flore, Jeanne, 13, 90, 99, 114–15 n.24; *Contes Amoureux*, 63, 73–74, 91, 95–96, 120 n.8

Florence, 63. *See also* Boccaccio, Giovanni
Foreword, 18
Form: marked, 91; unmarked, 91
Foucault, Michel: likeness, 46; primacy of the written word, 44. *See also* Likeness
Frame [*cornice*], 53, 80, 85, 88, 89, 99; Italian, 87
Frame of reference: narrator/reader, 38
Francis I, 37, 49, 91, 100, 108 n.25; and the Royal Family, 26–27, 33. *See also* Marguerite de Navarre
French custom, 70
Friendship, 53, 87. *See also* Montaigne, Michel de

Galen, 24
Garland, John of, 106 n.26
Gautier, Théophile, 12
Gender, marked, 99; unmarked, 99
Gender-district forms, 91
Generating circumstances, 43, 54, 79; adverse, 63; pleasurable, 63
Genette, Gérard, 11, 57–78, 104 n.1, 106 n.19, 113 n.7, 115 n. 1 and 5, 117 nn. 39 and 41; disclaimers, 37; prefatory functions, 15, 57–78, 79–80; *Seuils*, 11
Genre narratif bref, 14
Glidden, Hope, 105 n.12
Goals: didactic, 102
Good faith: open mind, 44, 86
Goodman, Nelson, 113 n.8
Good reading: setting up, 15
Goodwill, 107 n.18. See also *Captatio benevolentia*
Grandes et inestimables Chroniques de l'énorme géant Gargantua, 67. *See also* Rabelais, François
Greek and Latin theater: *parodo* or *parodus*, 12
Guenelec, 97
Guyon, 71

Hadrian, 70
Harsh laws of nature, 91
Headings, 72
Hearsay, 61
Hegel, 104 n.4
Hélisenne de Crenne, 73, 90, 91, 95, 96, 99, 100; *aux lisantes*, 17

Henle, Paul, 113n.6
Henri III, 109n.37, 118n.12. *See also* Marguerite de Navarre
Heraclides, 70
Hircan, 74, 99
Historian: parody, 111n.10
History: allusions to historic events, 33; ambiguity, 45, branch of literature, 45; collective memory, 34; details, 41; epic form, 34; generate narration, 36; goal, 34; grounding in, 33, 42, 53, 80, 81, 88, 100; *hic et nunc*, 37; historic personalities, 33; incite to right action, 45; inscribed in fiction, 108n.25; narrative form, 343; silhouetted events, 45; specificity, 38
History and fiction: interrelationship, 15
Homer, 23, 77
Horace, 27, 73; goals for poetry, 24; instruct and please, 108n.18
Horizon of expectation, 48, 49, 114n.12. *See also* Jauss, Hans Robert
Human behavior, 113n.35
Hunt, Tony, 11, 19, 106n.23
Hypogram, 109n.33. *See also* Riffaterre, Michael

Iliad, 97
Incipit, 83, 87; Medieval romances, 23; prologue to *Gargantua*, 22
Indiction, 112n.31
Innovation: *jeu de paume*, 43
Intellect: appropriated by women, 98
Interaction: text and reader, 86
Interpretation: allegorical, 47. *See also* Allegory
Intertextuality: intertext, 30–31, 109n.31; intertextual reference, 26
Invention [*inventio*], 88; boundaries, 50; definition, 34; downplayed, 36; goal, 34
Invitation to readers, 85

Jauss, Hans Robert, 114n.12. *See also* Horizon of expectation
Jeanneret, Michel, 101, 121n.5
Jenny, Laurent, 26
Joukovsky, Françoise, 112n.29
Jourda, Pierre, 84

Kasprzyk, Krystyna, 38
Kotin, Armine Avakian, 110n.6

Labé, Louise, 13, 90, 95, 99; *Débat de Folie et d'Amour*, 28–31, 91–95
La Boétie, Etienne, 63, 115n.26; displacement, 53–54; *La Servitude volontaire*, 53–54. *See also* Montaigne, Michel de
La Charité Raymond, 47, 114n.11
Ladulfi, Leon, 39; anagram of Noël du Fail, 17. *See also* Du Fail, Noël
La Jarte, Philippe de, 99, 108n.25, 121n.15
Language: poetic function, 114n.12; practical function, 114n.12
Lanham, Richard A., 111n.14
Larkin, Neil M., 86
La Sale, Antoine de, 108n.21
Latinini, Brunetto, 16, 48, 111n.16, 112n.28; *Li Livres dou trésor*, 13
Laughter, 76
Le Maçon, Antoine: translator of Boccaccio's *Decameron*, 17, 80
Le Picard, Philippe, 13. *See also* D'Alcripe, Philippe
Le Poulchre de la Motte Messemé, François, 14, 91; *Les Passetemps*, 63, 69
Likeness: analogy, 46; convenience, 46; emulation [*aemulatio*], 46; sympathy, 46
Limen, 86
Liminary conventions, 13
Liminary devices, 12
Liminary pages, 12
Liminary strategies, 14, 15; subversion, 101
Liminary style, 14
Linguistic register, 82
Link between reading and writing, 114n.11
Literary production, 62; compiler, 25; innovation, 24–25; therapy, 59; women, 30
Livingston, Charles H., 111n.18
Logos: speech, 18
Longarine, 59
Lorraine, 36
Louis XI, 36
Louis XII, 43
Ludic intention, 89
Lusignan, château de, 88
Lustrum, 112n.31
Lydgate, Barry, 32, 101

INDEX 133

Macro-function: anticipating narration, 80; creating a narrative screen, 80, 81
Marguerite of Austria, 43
Marguerite de Navarre, 13, 17, 18, 58, 91, 100, 108n.25; authority, 27; *L'Heptaméron*, 26–27, 33, 59, 61, 66, 74, 80, 88, 90–91, 99–100; Parlamente, 26. See also *L'Heptaméron*
Martin, Henri-Jean, 12
Mathieu-Castellani, Gisèle, 113n.35
Matière, 20
Medieval preachers, 102
Medieval rhetoric: generating circumstances, 25
Medieval romance, 19, 40, 108n.28, 111n.17
Medieval treatises, 19
Mélusine, 88
Memory, 53
Metacommentary: writing prologues, 79
Metaphor: agricultural, 27–28, 53; artisinal, 52–53; aviary, 60; bactrian camel, 50; *cellier*, 111n.13; chestnut, 55; commercial, 25, 38, 50, 51, 56, 58, 62, 66–67, 114n.18; currency, 42; culinary, 65, 71; definition, 55; Diogenes, 48; enigma, 55; fashion, 51, 58; father, 77; fictional, 45; fruit, 60; godfather/godson, 54, 55–56; individual appropriation, 24; liminary, 15, 54; marrow bone, 67; nature, 39; metaphor, 53, 87; parent/child, 56; power to suggest, 47; publication, 55; recycling new material, 47; schoolboy, 54; setting up a good reading, 50; Silenus box, 47; symbol, 46–47; two-colored slave, 50; theatrical, 40; writing, 23
Metonymy, 53
Metz, 22, 36, 111n.18
Meun, Jean de, 19, 21
Minerve, madame, 90, 91, 95, 114n.24
Minnis, A. J., 11, 19, 107n.10
Monologic/dialogic, 121n.15
Montaigne, Michel de, 45, 47, 105n.12, 115n.26, 118n.12; *au lecteur*, 31–32, 68, 86, 101; audience, 118n.9; "Des cannibales," 87; *Essais*, 12, 14, 53–54, 62; mortgaging metaphor, 56, 89, 109n.36; self-portrait, 60, 68, 118n.12; writing as compensatory exercise, 63

Motives for writing: comfort others, 31; record the wisdom of the village elders, 31; relaxation, 78; self-interest, 96; women's equality, 31
Muse: Christian, 97; classical, 97; feminine, 101
Mute state: men, 93; women, 93
Myth: definition, 48

Narration as remedy: laughter, 38
Narration versus exposition, 85
Narrative: coherence, 35; plausibility, 35, 45; packaging, 102; pact, 61, 62
Narrator, 21; accuracy of transcription, 39; authentication of events; oath of veracity, 43; primary, 99; sources, 24
Narrator/reader: fictional contract, 44
Nelson, William, 34, 67, 111n.10, 117n.32
Neoplatonism, 69
Nicolas de Troyes, 111n.13; *Le Grand Parangon des Nouvelles Nouvelles*, 37, 64
Norton, Glynn P., 111n.7
Nostradamus, 42
Nouvelle: definition, 13, 57, 110n.6; Medieval, 33; new look, 35; newsworthy, 13, 35; recent past, 13, 35, 41. See also Conte

Ollier, Marie-Louise, 11, 19, 20, 106–7n.6
Omission: male reader, 97
Opacity of the written word, 72
Opposition: exposition and narration, 102
Oral transmission, 17–18, 38; hearsay, 37
Origin of Medieval prologue, 19–20
Ovid, 23, 84

Pandora, 49
Pantagruel, 83–84
Pantagruélisme, 50, 111n.21
Paratext, 12; definition, 11, 104n.1. See also Genette, Gerard
Paratonnerre, 66, 71
Parlamente, 59, 88, 99
Parole du père, 118n.42
Paul, Saint, 98
Peace of Saint-Germain, 40
Peirce, C. S.: metaphor, 46

Performance objective, 102
Perigraphy, 117n.38; definition, 73
Pérouse, Gabriel A., 14, 88, 112n.24, 117n.34
Perrault, Charles: *Griseldis, Peau d'âne, Souhaits ridicules*, 103
Personal pronouns: marked for gender/unmarked for gender, 92–93
Philosophical treatises: prologues to, 81
Piccolomini, 106n.23
Plague, 80; Florence, 17
Plaisantin, 75, 85
Plato, 24, 27, 58; intertext, 47
Play: *jeu de paume*, 43, 81, 89; truth and fiction, 57
Plutarch, 17, 34, 77. See also Amyot, Jacques
Point of view, 91
Poissenot, Bénigne, 13; *L'Esté*, 60–61, 62, 77, 78; intention, 78; prefatory labels, 77
Poitiers, 51, 66, 90
Poitou/Poitevins, 59
Politian, 23
Portrait: incarnational, 32; Montaigne, 47; self, 32, 53–54, 87
Praise: inflated, 68
Preamble: Des Périers, Bonaventure, 12, 25
Preface: *auctoriale*, 115n.1; definition, 106n.19; elusive, 117n.41; as genre or sub-genre, 11; *originale*, 115n.1; problematic role, 79; reductive, 104n.4; superfluous, 104n.4
Prefaces to theoretical texts: Medieval, 102; Renaissance, 102
Préfacière, 95, 98
Préfaciers: Renaissance, 47, 69, 102
Prefatory discourse: limitations, 102
Prefatory functions, 57, 85, 102; advertisement for other works, 73, 84; attention [*attentio*], 15, 23, 41, 108n.18; benefits, 59; blame, 44, 61, 65; boosting morale, 59; bridging the gap, 79–89; describing approach, 48; eye witness, 27, 35, 39; goodwill, 15, 23, 41, 49; guiding reader reception, 50; humility oath [*excusatio propter infirmitatem*], 16, 32, 37, 52, 60, 96, 100, 120–21n.13; importance of work, 45, 57, 63; incite to virtuous action, 41, innovation, 47, 57, 58–59; instruct, 24, 61, 67, 73, 82, 85, 103; interest, 15, 108n.18; narrating conditions of production, 48; oath of veracity, 27, 32, 35, 36, 41, 41–42, 43, 57, 61, 62, 63, 68, 74, 88; originality, 26; please, 24, 41, 42, 43, 44, 51, 61, 67, 73, 74–76, 82, 85, 95; relieve sorrow, 120n.11; right disposition [*docilitas*], 23, 49; self-advertisement, 21; set work in context, 72; show familiar, 51; setting up a good reading, 47, 57, 63, 81, 89, 113n.7; simplicity, 61; unity, 57, 61; verisimilitude, 111n.7
Prefatory goals: delight, 36; instruct; possibility, 16
Prefatory labels: *avant-propos*, 15; *préambule*, 15; *préface*, 15; *proéme*, 15, 17; *avis au lecteur*, 15; *prolégomènes*, 15; *prologue*, 15; *aux bénévoles lecteurs*, 41; *au lecteur*, 17, 18, 101; *aux lecteurs*, 18, 91; *aux lisantes*, 18, 91; *aux liseurs*, 18
Prefatory strategies: Boccaccio, 95; equality, 99
Premierfait, Laurent de, 80
Preterition, 118n.43
Preview, 103
Primary narrative voice: unmarked, 99, 100
Prince, Gerald, 60, 63, 119n.18
Printed word: superiority, 115n.24
Printers: Aldus, 85, Estienne, 85, de Tournes, 85
Printing, 102; *conteurs*, 77; early years, 11; press, 22; Renaissance practices, 12
Production: book, 80; literary, 78, 88
Proem [*Proème, proemio*], 27, 80; *Decameron*, 30, definition, 16
Prologo in theater, 17
Prologue: Arthurian, 19, attention, 13, *chanson de geste*, 11, 28; classical origins, 32; covert, 48; definition, 16, goodwill, 13, 16; Greek theater, 28; Medieval, 11, 19, 32, 57, 104n.5, 106n.23; Medieval romances, 11, 28; Renaissance, 12, 57, 101; theater, 106n.23; threshold of fictional world, 33; translations, 81
Property: literary, 101

Proverbs/sententia, 50; *bene vivere et laetare*, 108 n.21; liminary, 75, 78
Pythagoras, 43

Quintilian: *Institutio oratoria*, 19

Rabelais, François, 17, 18, 24, 26, 47–50, 55, 58, 69, 85, 90, 102, 107 n.17, 111 n.21, 112 n.32; Alcofrybas, 23; corpus, 84; Couillatris, 24; elusive preface, 117 n.41; figures in the *Moyen de parvenir*, 43; *Gargantua*, 22, 23, 43, 47–48, 59, 67, 68, 70, 72–73, 74, 81, 82–83; laughter, 76; *Pantagruel*, 23, 59, 67, 68, 74, 81, 82–83; *Quart Livre*, 24, 75, 84; *Tiers Livre*, 23, 48–50, 59, 63, 64–65, 74, 83
Read, Kirk D., 91
Readers: benevolent, 98; exclusion, 98; expectations, 22; experience, 38; female, 64, 100; isolated, 101; male, 98; men and women, 90; modern, 45; noble, 98; Renaissance, 48; response, 64; restricted, 100; women, 64, 85, 90, 91, 96, 100
Real world: fictional signs, 45
Reason, Lady, 98
Reception: gender, 96; literary, 25, 88, 89; reader, 19, 50, 63, 64, 66, 107 n.17
Récit, 85
Recueils bigarrés, 69
Regalado, Nancy, 41
Religious wars, 39, 59, 112 n.28
Remigius of Auxerre, 19
Renaissance: French, 13; perception, 46
Repertoire: exotic, 50; French, 51, 58; local, 26, 28, 38, 50, 58, 81
Resemblance: likeness, 113 n.1
Respect: women's right to speak, 99
Response: reader, 79
Reynolds-Cornell, Régine, 120 n.8
Rhetoric: classical, 57, 70; Medieval, 57
Rhetorica ad Herennium, 12–13, 19
Rhetorical goal: persuade, 47
Rhetorical play, 37
Rhetorical strategies: amplification, 59; clarity, 37; eloquence, 37; explaining a word by its opposite, 27
Ricoeur, Paul, 55, 113 nn. 6 and 8
Riffaterre, Michael: intertext, 30; 109 nn. 31 and 33
Rigolot, François, 91, 105 n.9, 115 n.26

Roman, 20
Rules governing artistic space, 102
Russian formalists, 80

Saffredent, 99
Said, Edward, 63
Sample [*échantillon*], 84
Sampling, 75, 103
Schultz, James A., 11, 19, 106 n.26
Screen, narrative, 87
Self-authorization, 21. *See also* Authorization
Self-effacement, 20
Self-expression: equality, 99; right to, 99
Self-reflection, 110 n.40
Semantic collision, 55
Seneca, 67
Sententia: bene vivere et laetari, 25
Showing versus telling, 103
Silenus box: *Gargantua*, 23, 47, 49–50, 67, 114 n.10
Situational indices, 102
Socrates, 23, 43–44, 112 n.32, 114 n.10; description, 47
Sodom and Gomorrah, 82
Sources, 20–21; adaptations, 84
Sozzi, Lionello, 25
Specularity, 83
Speech: clear, 89; discreet/indiscreet, 96; transgressive, 96
Speech act: calling attention, 105 n.9
Speech act theory: application, 12
Spinning motif, 31. *See also* Boccaccio, Giovanni; Labé, Louise
Storytellers: *devisants*, 99; Italian, 15; Renaissance, 13, 15, 72; skepticism of, 79; tricks of the chroniclers, 35; women, 101
Storytelling: like alchemy, 42
Studia humanitatis, 20
Style: epistolary, 86; humble, 39, 69; high, 39, 69
Symmetry, 48
Symposium, 23, 89, 121 n.5

Tabourot, Estienne, 12, 14, 17
Tantalus, 49
Tense: play, 21
Testimony: oral, 62
Thomas Aquinas, Saint, 19
Tiraqueau, André, 24
Titling system, 60

Todorov, Tzvetan, 105n.9
Tone, 82
Topics of how, 64–78; choice of public, 63; classification by genre, 63; commentary on title, 63, 68, 70–71, 83; contextual hints, 63; declaration of intention, 73–77, 83; defining genre, 68; intention, 63; order, 71; ward off potential criticism, 83
Topics of why, 57–64; argument *a contrario*, 60, benefits, 59; importance, 59; novelty, 58; triviality, 60; truth, 61; unity, 61
Trait saillant [surprise twist], 38, 58, 112n.23
Transition to main text, 79
Translations: classical texts, 102
Translatio studii, 28
Transmission: oral, 115n.24
Truce: motive for writing, 36, 37
Trust, 62
Truth, 34, 36; illusion of, 41
Typology: Medieval prologues, 108n.22, 115n.1

Unauthorized editions, 63
Ungrammaticality: definition, 30, 109n.31
Unity of time, 81
Utterance: constative and performative, 105n.9

Value: entertainment, 82; intellectual, 82; of writing, 93
Verisimilitude, 81, 118n.7; test of, 45
Versants, 11
Vianey, Jean, 14
Vigneulles, Philippe de: *Les Cent Nouvelles Nouvelles*, 13, 21–22, 36–37, 50, 59, 61–62, 64, 69, 81, 96, 111n.17
Virgil, 27
Virgin Mary, Mother of Christ, 96–97
Voice: individual, 101

Weimann, Robert, 22, 106n.6
White, Hayden, 35; metaphor, 46. *See also* Metaphor
Winn, Colette, 110n.1, 111n.14
Wittig, Monique, 91
Women's discourse, 15
Word: spoken and written, 102
Writing: response to adversity, 59
Written word: primacy of, 44

Xenophon, 24, 58

Yver, Jacques, 13; genesis, 77; humility oath, 77; goals, 78; *Le Printemps*, 39–41, 52–53, 59, 62, 63, 65–66, 77, 80, 88, 89, 112n.28, 120n.11

Zink, Michel, 11, 19, 107n.6, 108n.28
Zumthor, Paul, 102